THE GOETIA

THE LESSER KEY OF SOLOMON THE KING

Translated by S. L. MACGREGOR MATHERS

Edited with Introduction and Commentary by ALEISTER CROWLEY

The Goetia: The Lesser Key of Solomon the King
Translated by S. L. MacGregor Mathers
Edited with Introduction and Commentary by Aleister Crowley

Print ISBN 13: 978-1-4209-7325-9

This edition copyright © 2021. Digireads.com Publishing.

All rights reserved. No part of this publication may be reproduced, distributed, or transmitted in any form or by any means, including photocopying, recording, or other electronic or mechanical methods, without the prior written permission of the publisher, except in the case of brief quotations embodied in critical reviews and certain other noncommercial uses permitted by copyright law.

Cover Image: a detail of "The First Experiment" (oil on canvas), by Antoine Francois Saint-Aubert (1715-88) / Bridgeman Images.

Please visit *www.digireads.com*

GOETIA

ΕΠΙΚΑΛΟΥΜΑΙ ΣΕ ΤΟΝ ΕΝ ΤΩ ΚΕΝΕΩ ΠΝΕΥΜΑΤΙ, ΔΕΙΝΟΝ, ΑΟΡΑΤΟΝ, ΠΑΝΤΟΚΡΑΤΟΡΑ, ΘΕΟΝ ΘΕΩΝ, ΦΘΕΡΟΠΟΙΟΝ, ΚΑΙ ΕΡΗΜΟΠΟΙΟΝ, Ο ΜΙΣΩΝ ΟΙΚΙΑΝ ΕΥΣΤΑΘΟΥΣΑΝ, ΩΣ ΕΞΕΒΡΑΣΘΗΣ ΕΚ ΤΗΣ ΑΙΓΥΠΤΙΟΥ ΚΑΙ ΕΞΩ ΧΩΡΑΣ.

ΕΠΟΝΟΜΑΣΘΗΣ Ο ΠΑΝΤΑ ΡΗΣΣΩΝ ΚΑΙ ΜΗ ΝΙΚΩΜΕΝΟΣ.

ΕΠΙΚΑΛΟΥΜΑΙ ΣΕ ΤΥΦΩΝ ΣΗΘ ΤΑΣ ΣΑΣ ΜΑΝΤΕΙΑΣ ΕΠΙΤΕΛΩ, ΟΤΙ ΕΠΙΚΑΛΟΥΜΑΙ ΣΕ ΤΟ ΣΟΝ ΑΥΘΕΝΤΙΚΟΝ ΣΟΥ ΟΝΟΜΑ ΕΝ ΟΙΣ ΟΥ ΔΥΝΗ ΠΑΡΑΚΟΥΣΑΙ ΙΩΕΡΒΗΘ, ΙΩΠΑΚΕΡΒΗΘ, ΙΩΒΟΛΧΩΣΗΘ, ΙΩΠΑΤΑΘΝΑΞ, ΙΩΣΩΡΩ, ΙΩΝΕΒΟΥΤΟΣΟΥΑΛΗΘ, ΑΚΤΙΩΦΙ, ΕΡΕΣΧΙΓΑΛ, ΝΕΒΟΠΟΩΑΛΗΘ, ΑΒΕΡΑΜΕΝΘΩΟΝ, ΛΕΡΘΕΞΑΝΑΞ, ΕΘΡΕΛΥΩΘ, ΝΕΜΑΡΕΒΑ, ΑΕΜΙΝΑ, ΟΛΟΝ ΗΚΕ ΜΟΙ ΚΑΙ ΒΑΔΙΣΟΝ ΚΑΙ ΚΑΤΕΒΑΛΕ ΤΟΝ ΔΕΙΝΟΝ ΜΑΘΕΡΣ. ΡΙΓΕΙ ΚΑΙ ΠΥΡΕΙΩ ΑΥΤΟΣ ΗΔΙΚΗΣΕΝ ΤΟΝ ΑΝΘΡΩΠΟΝ ΚΑΙ ΤΟ ΑΙΜΑ ΤΟΥ ΦΥΩΝΟΣ ΕΞΕΧΥΣΕΝ ΠΑΡ' ΕΑΥΤΩ.

ΔΙΑ ΤΟΥΤΟ ΤΑΥΤΑ ΠΟΙΕΩ ΚΟΙΝΑ.

```
K O D S E LI M
O
H
A
B
I           O
M        O K
```

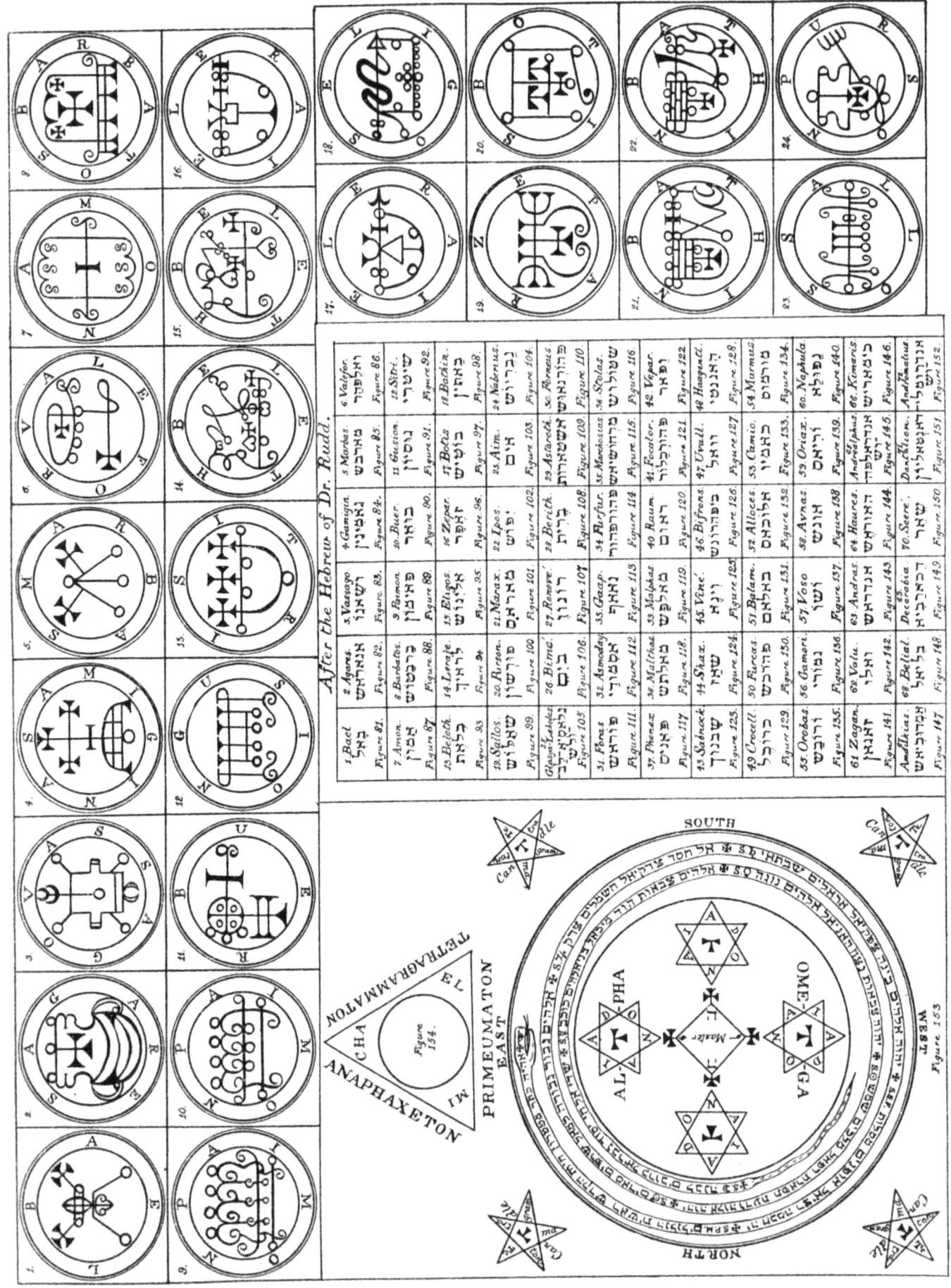

THE BOOK OF THE
GOETIA

OF

SOLOMON THE KING

TRANSLATED INTO THE ENGLISH TONGUE BY A
DEAD HAND

AND

ADORNED WITH DIVERS OTHER MATTERS GERMANE
DELIGHTFUL TO THE WISE

THE WHOLE

EDITED, VERIFIED, INTRODUCED AND COMMENTED

BY

ALEISTER CROWLEY

PREFATORY NOTE.

A.G.R.C.   *A.R.C.G.*

THIS translation of the First Book of the "Lemegeton" (now for the first time made accessible to English adepts and students of the Mysteries) was done, after careful collation and edition, from numerous MSS. in Hebrew, Latin, French and English, by G. H. Fra. D.D.C.F., by the order of the Secret Chief of the Rosicrucian Order.[1] The G. H. Fra., having succumbed unhappily to the assaults of the Four Great Princes (acting notably under Martial influences), it seemed expedient that the work should be brought to its conclusion by another hand. The investigations of a competent Skryer into the house of our unhappy Fra., confirmed this divination; neither our Fra. nor his Hermetic Mul. were there seen; but only the terrible shapes of the evil Adepts S.V.A.[2] and

---

[1] Mr. A. E. Waite writes ("Real History of the Rosicrucians," p. 426): "I beg leave to warn my readers that all persons who proclaim themselves to be Rosicrucians are simply members of pseudo-fraternities, and that there is that difference between their assertion and the fact of the case in which the essence of a lie consists!"

It is within the Editor's personal knowledge that Mr. Waite was (and still is probably) a member of a society claiming to be the R.C. fraternity.

As Mr. Waite constantly hints in his writings that he is in touch with initiated centres, I think the syllogism, whose premisses are given above, is fair, if not quite formal.—ED.

[2] It was owing to our Fra. receiving this S.V.A. as his Superior, and giving up the Arcana of our Fraternity into so unhallowed a power, that We decided no longer to leave Our dignity and authority in the hands of one who could be thus easily imposed upon. (For by a childish and easy magical trick did S.V.A. persuade D.D.C.F. of that lie.)

H., whose original bodies having been sequestered by Justice, were no longer of use to them. On this we stayed no longer Our Hand; but withdrawing Ourselves, and consulting the Rota, and the Books M. and Q. did decide to ask Mr. Aleister Crowley,[1] a poet, and skilled student of Magical Lore, and an expert Kabbalist, to complete openly that which had been begun in secret.[2] This is that which is written: "His Bishoprick let another take." And again: "Oculi Tetragrammaton." This is also that which is said: "Nomen Secundum קרע שטן refertur ad *Gebhurah*; qui est *Rex* secundus, quo moriente *delabebantur Posteriora Matris*, unde *Bittul* atque Corruptio *Achurajim Patris et Matris* hoc indigitatur."

And so saying we wish you well.

> Ex Deo Nascimur.
> In Jesu Morimur.
> Per S.S. Reviviscimus.

Given forth from our Mountain of A.,
    this day of C.C. 1903 A.D.

---

[1] The task of editing the MSS. thus placed in my hands has proved practically a sinecure. The original translator and editor had completed his work so efficiently that very little was left for me to do beyond undertaking the business transactions connected with it, reading the proofs, and deciphering, with transliteration from the Enochian characters, the "Angelic" version of Perdurabo, from the priceless MS. entrusted to me.—ED.

[2] He that is appointed to complete in secret that which had been begun openly is R.R., and to be heard of at the care of the Editor.

PRELIMINARY INVOCATION.

Thee I invoke, the Bornless one.
Thee, that didst create the Earth and the Heavens:
Thee, that didst create the Night and the Day.
Thee, that didst create the Darkness and the Light.
Thou art Osorronophris: Whom no man hath seen at any time.
Thou art Iabas:
Thou art Iapōs:
Thou hast distinguished between the Just and the Unjust.
Thou didst make the female and Male.
Thou didst produce the Seed and the Fruit.
Thou didst form Men to love one another, and to hate one another.

    I am Mosheh Thy Prophet, unto Whom Thou didst commit Thy Mysteries, the Ceremonies of Ishrael:
    Thou didst produce the moist and the dry, and that which nourisheth all created Life.
    Hear Thou Me, for I am the Angel of Paphrō Osorronophris: this is Thy True Name, handed down to the Prophets of Ishrael.

א

Hear Me:—
Ar: Thiao: Rheibet: Atheleberseth:
A: Blatha: Abeu: Ebeu: Phi:
Thitasoe: Ib: Thiao.

Hear Me, and make all Spirits subject unto Me: so that every Spirit of the Firmament and of the Ether: upon the Earth and under the Earth: on dry Land and in the Water: of Whirling Air, and of rushing Fire: and every Spell and Scourge of God may be obedient unto Me.

ש

I invoke Thee, the Terrible and Invisible God: Who dwellest in the Void Place of the Spirit:—

Arogogorobrao: Sothou:
Modorio: Phalarthao: Doo: Apé, The Bornless One:
Hear Me: etc.

ם

Hear me:—
Roubriao: Mariodam: Balbnabaoth: Assalonai: Aphniao: I:
Thoteth: Abrasar: Aëöoü: Ischure, Mighty and Bornless One!
Hear me: etc.

ת

I invoke Thee:—
　Ma: Barraio: Jōēl: Kotha:
　Athorēbalō: Abraoth:
Hear Me: etc.

אמן

Hear me!
Aōth: Abaōth: Basum: Isak:
Sabaoth: Iao:

This is the Lord of the Gods:
This is the Lord of the Universe:
This is He Whom the Winds fear.

This is He, Who having made Voice by His Commandment, is Lord of All Things; King, Ruler and Helper.

Hear Me, etc.

Hear Me:—

Ieou: Pûr: Iou: Pûr: Iaôt: Iaeô: Ioou: Abrasar: Sabriam: Do: Uu: Adonaie: Ede: Edu: Angelos ton Theon: Aniala Lai: Gaia: Ape: Diathanna Thorun.

I Am He! the Bornless Spirit! having sight in the Feet: Strong, and the Immortal Fire!

I Am He! the Truth!

I Am He! Who hate that evil should be wrought in the World!

I am He, that lighteneth and thundereth.

I am He, from whom is the Shower of the Life of Earth:

I am He, whose mouth ever flameth:

I am He, the Begetter and Manifester unto the Light:

I am He; the Grace of the World:

"The Heart Girt with a Serpent" is My Name!

Come Thou forth, and follow Me: and make all Spirits subject unto Me so that every Spirit of the Firmament, and of the Ether: upon the Earth and under the Earth: on dry land, or in the Water: of whirling Air or of rushing Fire: and every Spell and Scourge of God, may be obedient unto me!

Iao: Sabao:

Such are the Words!

The Initiated Interpretation of Ceremonial Magic.[1]

IT is loftily amusing to the student of magical literature who is not quite a fool—and rare is such a combination!—to note the criticism directed by the Philistine against the citadel of his science. Truly, since our childhood has ingrained into us not only literal belief in the Bible, but also substantial belief in Alf Laylah wa Laylah,[2] and only adolescence can cure us, we are only too liable, in the rush and energy of dawning manhood, to overturn roughly and rashly both these classics, to regard them both on the same level, as interesting documents from the standpoint of folk-lore and anthropology, and as nothing more.

Even when we learn that the Bible, by a profound and minute study of the text, may be forced to yield up Qabalistic arcana of cosmic scope and importance, we are too often slow to apply a similar restorative to the companion volume, even if we are the lucky holders of Burton's veritable edition.

To me, then, it remains to raise the Alf Laylah wa Laylah into its proper place once more.

I am not concerned to deny the objective reality of all "magical" phenomena; if they are illusions, they are at least as real as many unquestioned facts of daily life; and, if we follow Herbert Spencer, they are at least evidence of some cause.[3]

Now, this fact is our base. What is the cause of my illusion of seeing a spirit in the triangle of Art?

Every smatterer, every expert in psychology, will answer: "That cause lies in your brain."

[1] Introductory Essay. By Aleister Crowley.
[2] "A thousand and one Nights" commonly called "Arabian Nights".
[3] This, incidentally, is perhaps the greatest argument we possess, pushed to its extreme, against the Advaitist theories.

English children (*pace* the Education Act) are taught that the Universe lies in infinite Space; Hindu children, in the Akaśa, which is the same thing.

Those Europeans who go a little deeper learn from Fichte, that the phenomenal Universe is the creation of the Ego; Hindus, or Europeans studying under Hindu Gurus, are told, that by Akaśa is meant the Chitakaśa. The Chitakaśa is situated in the "Third Eye," *i.e.*, in the brain. By assuming higher dimensions of space, we can assimilate this fact to Realism; but we have no need to take so much trouble.

This being true for the ordinary Universe, that all sense-impressions are dependent on changes in the brain,[1] we must include illusions, which are after all sense-impressions as much as "realities" are, in the class of "phenomena dependent on brain-changes."

Magical phenomena, however, come under a special sub-class, since they are willed, and their cause is the series of "real" phenomena called the operations of ceremonial Magic.

These consist of

(1) Sight.
>> The circle, square, triangle, vessels, lamps, robes, implements, etc.

(2) Sound.
>> The invocations.

(3) Smell.
>> The perfumes.

(4) Taste.
>> The Sacraments.

(5) Touch.
>> As under (1).

(6) Mind.
>> The combination of all these and reflection on their significance.

These unusual impressions (1-5) produce unusual brain-changes; hence their summary (6) is of unusual kind. Its projection back into the apparently phenomenal world is therefore unusual.

---

[1] Thought is a secretion of the brain (Weissmann). Consciousness is a function of the brain (Huxley).

Herein then consists the reality of the operations and effects of ceremonial magic,[1] and I conceive that the apology is ample, so far as the "effects" refer only to those phenomena which appear to the magician himself, the appearance of the spirit, his conversation, possible shocks from imprudence, and so on, even to ecstasy on the one hand, and death or madness on the other.

But can any of the effects described in this our book Goetia be obtained, and if so, can you give a rational explanation of the circumstances? Say you so?

I can, and will.

The spirits of the Goetia are portions of the human brain.

Their seals therefore represent (Mr. Spencer's projected cube) methods of stimulating or regulating those particular spots (through the eye).

The names of God are vibrations calculated to establish:

(*a*) General control of the brain. (Establishment of functions relative to the subtle world.)

(*b*) Control over the brain in detail. (Rank or type of the Spirit.)

(*c*) Control of one special portion. (Name of the Spirit.)

The perfumes aid this through smell. Usually the perfume will only tend to control a large area; but there is an attribution of perfumes to letters of the alphabet enabling one, by a Qabalistic formula, to spell out the Spirit's name.

I need not enter into more particular discussion of these points; the intelligent reader can easily fill in what is lacking.

If, then, I say, with Solomon:

"The Spirit Cimieries teaches logic," what I mean is:

"Those portions of my brain which subserve the logical faculty may be stimulated and developed by following out the processes called 'The Invocation of Cimieries.'"

And this is a purely materialistic rational statement; it is independent of any objective hierarchy at all. Philosophy has nothing to say; and Science can only suspend judgment, pending a proper and methodical investigation of the facts alleged.

---

[1] Apart from its value in obtaining one-pointedness. On this subject the curious may consult my בראשית.

Unfortunately, we cannot stop there. Solomon promises us that we can (1) obtain information; (2) destroy our enemies; (3) understand the voices of nature; (4) obtain treasure; (5) heal diseases, etc. I have taken these five powers at random; considerations of space forbid me to explain all.

(1) Brings up facts from sub-consciousness.

(2) Here we come to an interesting fact. It is curious to note the contrast between the noble means and the apparently vile ends of magical rituals. The latter are disguises for sublime truths. "To destroy our enemies" is to realize the illusion of duality, to excite compassion.

(Ah! Mr. Waite, the world of Magic is a mirror, wherein who sees muck is muck.)

(3) A careful naturalist will understand much from the voices of the animals he has studied long. Even a child knows the difference of a cat's miauling and purring. The faculty may be greatly developed.

(4) Business capacity may be stimulated.

(5) Abnormal states of the body may be corrected, and the involved tissues brought back to tone, in obedience to currents started from the brain.

So for all other phenomena. There is no effect which is truly and necessarily miraculous.

Our Ceremonial Magic fines down, then, to a series of minute, though of course empirical, physiological experiments, and whoso will carry them through intelligently need not fear the result.

I have all the health, and treasure, and logic, I need; I have no time to waste. "There is a lion in the way." For me these practices are useless; but for the benefit of others less fortunate I give them to the world, together with this explanation of, and apology for, them.

I trust that the explanation will enable many students who have hitherto, by a puerile objectivity in their view of the question, obtained no results, to succeed; that the apology may impress upon our scornful men of science that the study of the bacillus should give place to that of the baculum, the little to the great—how great one only realizes when one identifies the wand with the Mahalingam, up which Brahma flew at the rate of 84,000 yojanas a second for 84,000 mahakalpas;[1] down which Vishnu flew at the rate of

[1] The Phallus of Shiva the Destroyer. It is really identical with the Qabalistic "Middle Pillar" of the "Tree of Life".

84,000 crores of yojanas a second for 84,000 crores of mahakalpas—yet neither reached an end.

But I reach an end.

BOLESKINE HOUSE,
Foyers, N.B., *July*, 1903.

NOTE.—I had intended in this place to devote a little attention to the edition (save the mark) of the "Goetia" produced by Mr. A. E. Waite in the "Book of Black Magic."

But a fresh perusal of that work reveals it to be such a farrago of twenty-fifth-rate shoddy schoolboy journalism that disgust compels me to refrain. I may merely mention that the letterpress is garbled and the seals abominably drawn. To give one concrete example; on p. 202 Mr. Waite observes:

"This" (that the compiler of the Lemegeton was acquainted with the N. T.) "is proved by the references in the Third Conjuration to the Living Creatures of the Apocalypse."

There is no such reference!

In the Second Conjuration, for I have corrected Mr. Waite's careless blunder, there is a reference to Living Creatures; there is also a reference to the same beings in the Apocalypse.

The argument then stands:

The Book of Chronicles refers to King Solomon (unknown date).

Mr. Waite refers to King Solomon (1898),

Therefore,

The author of the Book of Chronicles was acquainted with Mr. Waite's book.[1]

We will conclude by condoling with the author of the Book of Chronicles.

---

[1] Even apart from this, if Living Creatures are really existent things—which the name would suggest—the argument stands:

The Rig-Veda,
The Old Testament,
The Insidecompletuar Britanniaware,
The Sword of Song

all refer to the Sun.

∴ there is a common source in literature.

Mr. Waite's fallacy is all very well, though, for people who have never kept Living Creatures, nor even made a fourth at Bridge.

LEMEGETON VEL CLAVICULA SALOMONIS REGIS.

THE PRELIMINARY DEFINITION OF MAGIC.[1]

MAGIC is the Highest, most Absolute, and most Divine Knowledge of Natural Philosophy, advanced in its works and wonderful operations by a right understanding of the inward and occult virtue of things; so that true Agents[2] being applied to proper Patients,[3] strange and admirable effects will thereby be produced. Whence magicians are profound and diligent searchers into Nature: they, because of their skill, know how to anticipate an effort,[4] the which to the vulgar shall seem to be a miracle.

Origen saith that the Magical Art doth not contain anything subsisting, but although it should, yet that it must not be Evil, or subject to contempt or scorn: and doth distinguish the *Natural Magic* from that which is *Diabolical*.

Apollonius Tyanaeus only exercised the *Natural Magic*, by the which he did perform wonderful things.

Philo Hebraeus saith that true Magic, by which we do arrive at the understanding of the Secret Works of Nature, is so far from being contemptible that the greatest Monarchs and Kings have studied it. Nay! among the Persians none might reign unless he was skilful in this GREAT ART.

This Noble Science often degenerateth, from *Natural* becometh *Diabolical*, and from *True Philosophy* turneth unto *Nigromancy*.[5] The which is wholly to be charged upon its followers, who, abusing or not being capable of that High and Mystical Knowledge do immediately hearken unto the temptations of *Sathan*, and are misled by him into the Study of the *Black*

---

[1] This Preliminary Definition of Magic is found in very few Codices, and is probably later than the body of the work.
[2] Or Actives. [3] Or Passives. [4] Or Effect.
[5] Or the Black Art, as distinct from mere Necromancy, or Divination by the Dead.

Art. Hence it is that Magic lieth under disgrace, and they who seek after it are vulgarly esteemed *Sorcerers.*

The Fraternity of the Rosie Crusians thought it not fit to style themselves Magicians, but rather Philosophers. And they be not ignorant Empiricks,[1] but learned and experienced Physicians, whose remedies be not only *Lawful* but *Divine.*

THE BRIEF INTRODUCTORY DESCRIPTION.

(N.B. This is taken from several MS. Codices, of which the four principal variations are here composed together in parallel columns as an example of the close agreement of the various texts of the Lemegeton.

For in the whole work the differences in the wording of the various Codices are not sufficient to require the constant giving of parallel readings; but except in the more ancient examples there is much deterioration in the Seals and Sigils, so that in this latter respect the more recent exemplars are not entirely reliable.)

CLAVICULA SALOMONIS REGIS,	THE WHOLE LEMEGETON OR CLAVICULA.	CLAVICULA SALOMONIS REGIS,	THE KEY OF SOLOMON.
which containeth all the Names, Offices, and Orders of all the Spirits that ever he had converse with, with the Seals and Characters to each Spirit and the manner of calling them forth to visible appearance:	Now this Book containeth all the Names, Orders, and Offices of all the Spirits with which Solomon ever conversed, the Seals and Characters belonging to each Spirit, and the manner of calling them forth to visible appearance:	which containeth all the Names, Offices, and Orders of all the Spirits with whom he ever held any converse; together with the Seals and Characters proper unto each Spirit, and the method of calling them forth to visible appearance:	which contains all the names, orders, and offices of all the Spirits that ever Solomon conversed with, together with the Seals and Characters belonging to each Spirit, and the manner of calling them forth to visible appearance:
In 5 parts, viz.:	Divided into 5 special Books or parts, viz.:	In 5 parts, viz.:	In 4 parts.
(1) THE FIRST PART is a Book of Evil Spirits, called GOETIA, showing how	(1) THE FIRST BOOK, or PART, which is a Book concerning Spirits of Evil, and	(1) THE FIRST PART is a Book of Evil Spirits, called GOETIA, showing how	(1) THE FIRST PART is a Book of Evil Spirits called GOETIA, showing how

---

[1] Or Quacks and Pretenders. Vide note on p. 10.

he bound up those Spirits, and used them in general things, whereby he obtained great fame.	which is termed THE GOETIA OF SOLOMON, sheweth forth his manner of binding these Spirits for use in things divers. And hereby did he acquire great renown.	he bound up those Spirits and used them in things general and several, whereby he obtained great fame.	he bound up those Spirits and used them in several things, whereby he obtained great fame.
(2) THE SECOND PART is a Book of Spirits, partly Evil and partly Good, which is named THEURGIA-GOETIA, all Aërial Spirits, etc.	(2) THE SECOND BOOK is one which treateth of Spirits mingled of Good and Evil Natures, the which is entitled THE THEURGIA-GOETIA, or the Magical Wisdom of the Spirits Aërial, whereof some do abide, but certain do wander and abide not.	(2) THE SECOND PART is a Book of Spirits partly Evil, and partly Good, which is called THEURGIA-GOETIA, all Aërial Spirits, etc.	(2.) THE SECOND PART is a Book of Spirits partly Good and partly Evil, which is named THEURGIA-GOETIA, all Aërial Spirits.
(3) THE THIRD PART is of Spirits governing the Planetary Hours, and what Spirits belong to every degree, of the Signs, and Planets in the Signs. Called the PAULINE ART, etc.	(3) THE THIRD BOOK, called ARS PAULINA, or THE ART PAULINE, treateth of the Spirits allotted unto every degree of the 360 Degrees of the Zodiac; and also of the Signs, and of the Planets in the Signs, as well as of the Hours.	(3) THE THIRD PART is of Spirits governing the Planetary Hours, and of what Spirits do belong to every Degree of the Signs, and of the Planets in the Signs. This is called the PAULINE ART, etc.	(3) THE THIRD PART is a Book governing the Planetary Houses, and what Spirits belong to every Degree of the Signs, and Planets in the Signs. Called the Pauline Art.
(4) THE FOURTH PART of this Book is called ALMADEL OF SOLOMON, which containeth those Spirits which govern the Four Altitudes, or the 360 Degrees of the Zodiac.	(4) THE FOURTH BOOK, called ARS ALMADEL SALOMONIS, or THE ART ALMADEL OF SOLOMON, concerneth those Spirits which be set over the Quaternary of the Altitudes.	(4) THE FOURTH PART of this Book is called ALMADEL OF SOLOMON, the which containeth those Spirits which do govern the Four Altitudes, or the 360 Degrees of the Zodiac.	(4) THE FOURTH PART is a Book called the ALMADEL OF SOLOMON, which contains Twenty Chief Spirits who govern the Four Altitudes, or the 360 Degrees of the Zodiac.
These two last Orders of Spirits are Good, and to be	These two last mentioned Books, the ART PAULINE and the	These two last Orders of Spirits are Good, and are called	These two last Orders of Spirits are Good, and called

sought for by Divine seeking, etc., and are called THEURGIA.	ART ALMADEL, do relate unto Good Spirits alone, whose knowledge is to be obtained through seeking unto the Divine. These two Books be also classed together under the Name of the First and Second Parts of the Book THEURGIA OF SOLOMON.	THEURGIA, and are to be sought for by Divine seeking, etc.	THEURGIA, and are to be sought after by Divine seeking.
(5) THE FIFTH PART is a Book of Orations and Prayers that Wise Solomon used upon the Altar in the Temple. The which is called ARS NOVA, which was revealed unto Solomon by that Holy Angel of God called MICHAEL; and he also received many brief Notes written with the Finger of God, which were declared to him by the said Angel with Claps of Thunder; without which Notes King Solomon had never obtained his great knowledge, for by them in a short time he knew all Arts and Sciences both Good and Bad: from these Notes it is called the NOTARY ART, etc.	(5) THE FIFTH BOOK of the Lemegeton is one of Prayers and Orations. The which Solomon the Wise did use upon the Altar in the Temple. And the titles hereof be ARS NOVA, the NEW ART, and ARS NOTARIA, the NOTARY ART. The which was revealed unto him by MICHAEL, that Holy Angel of God, in thunder and in lightning, and he further did receive by the aforesaid Angel certain Notes written by the Hand of God, without the which that Great King had never attained unto his great Wisdom, for thus he knew all things and all Sciences and Arts whether Good or Evil.	(5) THE FIFTH PART is a Book of Orations and Prayers which Wise Solomon did use upon the Altar in the Temple. The which is called ARS NOVA, the which was revealed to Solomon by that Holy Angel of God called Michael; and he also received many brief Notes written with the Finger of God, which were declared to him by the said Angel with Claps of Thunder; without which Notes King Solomon had never obtained his Great Wisdom, for by them in short time he gained Knowledge of all Arts and Sciences both Good and Bad; from these Notes it is called the NOTARY ART, etc.	These Most Sacred Mysteries were revealed unto Solomon.

Now in this Book LEMEGETON is contained the whole Art of King Solomon. And although there be many other Books that are said to be his, yet none is to be compared hereunto, for this containeth them all. Though there be titles with several other Names of the Book, as THE BOOK HELISOL, which is the very same with this last Book of Lemegeton called ARS NOVA or ARS NOTARIA, etc.

These Books were first found in the Chaldee and Hebrew Tongues at Jerusalem by a Jewish Rabbi; and by him put into the Greek language and thence into the Latin, as it is said.[1]

[1] The first only of these five books is here published: the astral opposition incidental to the publication of any magical writing is not to be blamed for this; but the engorgement of the translator in a matter of other import, as previously hinted. The true life of this man and his associates, with a veridic account of their researches into magical arts, etc., may be looked for in my forthcoming volume:

"History of the Order of the Golden Dawn." —ED.

GOETIA.

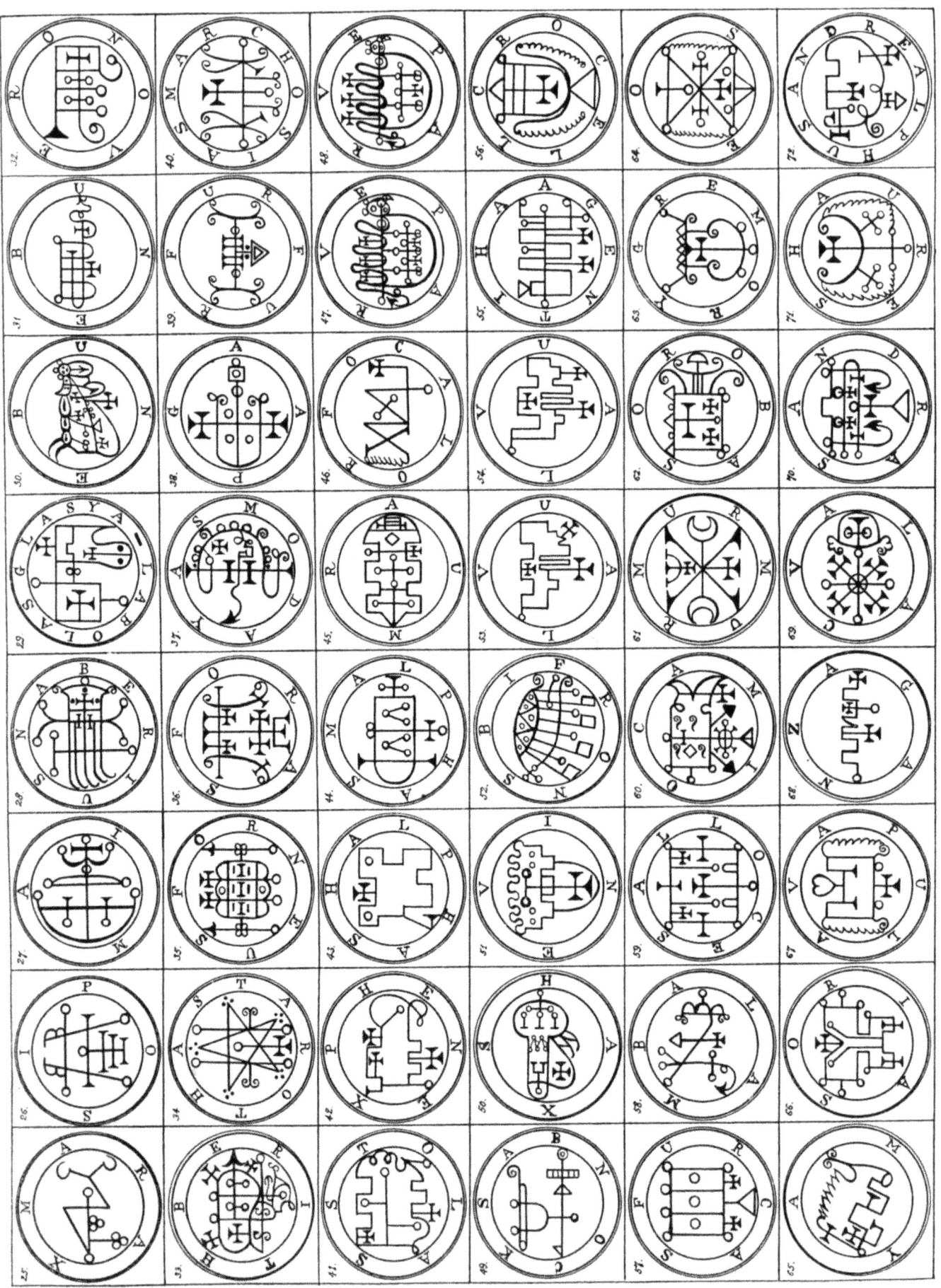

Shemhamphorash.

(1.) BAEL.—The First Principal Spirit is a King ruling in the East, called Bael. He maketh thee to go Invisible. He ruleth over 66 Legions of Infernal Spirits. He appeareth in divers shapes, sometimes like a Cat, sometimes like a Toad, and sometimes like a Man, and sometimes all these forms at once. He speaketh hoarsely. This is his character which is used to be worn as a Lamen before him who calleth him forth, or else he will not do thee homage.[1]

(2.) AGARES.—The Second Spirit is a Duke called Agreas, or Agares. He is under the Power of the East, and cometh up in the form of an old fair Man, riding upon a Crocodile, carrying a Goshawk upon his fist, and yet mild in appearance. He maketh them to run that stand still, and bringeth back runaways. He teaches all Languages or Tongues presently. He hath power also to destroy Dignities both Spiritual and Temporal, and causeth Earthquakes. He was of the Order of Virtues. He hath under his government 31 Legions of Spirits. And this is his Seal or Character which thou shalt wear as a Lamen before thee.

(3.) VASSAGO.—The Third Spirit is a Mighty Prince, being of the same nature as Agares. He is called Vassago. This Spirit is of a Good Nature, and his office is to declare things Past and to Come, and to discover all things Hid or Lost. And he governeth 26 Legions of Spirits, and this is his Seal.

(4.) SAMIGINA, or GAMIGIN.—The Fourth Spirit is Samigina, a Great Marquis. He appeareth in the form of a little Horse or Ass, and then into

---

[1] I am not responsible for this ultra-Arian confusion of persons.—ED.

Human shape doth he change himself at the request of the Master. He speaketh with a hoarse voice. He ruleth over 30 Legions of Inferiors. He teaches all Liberal Sciences, and giveth account of Dead Souls that died in sin. And his Seal is this, which is to be worn before the Magician when he is Invocator, etc.

(5.) MARBAS.—The fifth Spirit is Marbas. He is a Great President, and appeareth at first in the form of a Great Lion, but afterwards, at the request of the Master, he putteth on Human Shape. He answereth truly of things Hidden or Secret. He causeth Diseases and cureth them. Again, he giveth great Wisdom and Knowledge in Mechanical Arts; and can change men into other shapes. He governeth 36 Legions of Spirits. And his Seal is this, which is to be worn as aforesaid.

(6.) VALEFOR.—The Sixth Spirit is Valefor. He is a mighty Duke, and appeareth in the shape of a Lion with an Ass's Head, bellowing. He is a good Familiar, but tempteth them he is a familiar of to steal. He governeth 10 Legions of Spirits. His Seal is this, which is to be worn, whether thou wilt have him for a Familiar, or not.

(7.) AMON.—The Seventh Spirit is Amon. He is a Marquis great in power, and most stern. He appeareth like a Wolf with a Serpent's tail, vomiting out of his mouth flames of fire; but at the command of the Magician he putteth on the shape of a Man with Dog's teeth beset in a head like a Raven; or else like a Man with a Raven's head (simply). He telleth all things Past and to Come. He procureth feuds and reconcileth controversies between friends. He governeth 40 Legions of Spirits. His Seal is this which is to be worn as aforesaid, etc.

(8.) BARBATOS.—The Eighth Spirit is Barbatos. He is a Great Duke, and appeareth when the Sun is in Sagittary, with four noble Kings and their companies of great troops. He giveth understanding of the singing of Birds, and of the Voices of other creatures, such as the barking of Dogs. He breaketh the Hidden Treasures open that have been laid by the Enchantments of Magicians. He is of the Order of Virtues, of which some part he retaineth still; and he knoweth all things Past, and to Come, and conciliateth Friends and those that be in Power. He ruleth over 30 Legions of Spirits. His Seal of Obedience is this, the which wear before thee as aforesaid.

(9.) PAIMON.—The Ninth Spirit in this Order is Paimon, a Great King, and very obedient unto LUCIFER. He appeareth in the form of a Man sitting upon a Dromedary with a Crown most glorious upon his head. There goeth before him also an Host of Spirits, like Men with Trumpets and well sounding Cymbals, and all other sorts of Musical Instruments. He hath a great Voice, and roareth at his first coming, and his speech is such that the Magician cannot well understand unless he can compel him. This Spirit can teach all Arts and Sciences, and other secret things. He can discover unto thee what the Earth is, and what holdeth it up in the Waters; and what Mind is, and where it is; or any other thing thou mayest desire to know. He giveth Dignity, and confirmeth the same. He bindeth or maketh any man subject unto the Magician if he so desire it. He giveth good Familiars, and such as can teach all Arts. He is to be observed towards the West. He is of the Order of Dominations.[1] He hath under him 200 Legions of Spirits, and part of them are of the Order of Angels, and the other part of Potentates. Now if thou callest this Spirit Paimon alone, thou must make him some offering; and there will attend him two Kings called LABAL and ABALIM, and also other Spirits who be of the Order of Potentates in his Host, and 25 Legions. And those Spirits which be subject unto them are not always with them unless the Magician do compel them. His Character is this which must be worn as a Lamen before thee, etc.

(10.) BUER.—The Tenth Spirit is Buer, a Great President. He appeareth in Sagittary, and that is his shape when the Sun is there. He teaches Philosophy, both Moral and Natural, and the Logic Art, and also the Virtues of all Herbs and Plants. He healeth all distempers in man, and giveth good Familiars. He governeth 50 Legions of Spirits, and his Character of obedience is this, which thou must wear when thou callest him forth unto appearance.

(11.) GUSION.—The Eleventh Spirit in order is a great and strong Duke, called Gusion. He appeareth like a Xenopilus. He telleth all things, Past, Present, and to Come, and showeth the meaning and resolution of all questions thou mayest ask. He conciliateth and reconcileth friendships, and giveth Honour and Dignity unto any. He ruleth over 40 Legions of Spirits. His Seal is this, the which wear thou as aforesaid.

[1] Or Dominions, as they are usually termed.

(12.) SITRI.—The Twelfth Spirit is Sitri. He is a Great Prince, and appeareth at first with a Leopard's head and the Wings of a Gryphon, but after the command of the Master of the Exorcism he putteth on Human shape, and that very beautiful. He enflameth men with Women's love, and Women with Men's love; and causeth them also to show themselves naked if it be desired. He governeth 60 Legions of Spirits. His Seal is this, to be worn as a Lamen before thee, etc.

(13.) BELETH.—The Thirteenth Spirit is called Beleth (or Bileth, or Bilet). He is a mighty King and terrible. He rideth on a pale horse with trumpets and other kinds of musical instruments playing before him. He is very furious at his first appearance, that is, while the Exorcist layeth his courage; for to do this he must hold a Hazel Wand in his hand, striking it out towards the South and East Quarters, make a triangle, Δ, without the Circle, and then command him into it by the Bonds and Charges of Spirits as hereafter followeth. And if he doth not enter into the triangle, Δ, at your threats, rehearse the Bonds and Charms before him, and then he will yield Obedience and come into it, and do what he is commanded by the Exorcist. Yet he must receive him courteously because he is a Great King, and do homage unto him, as the Kings and Princes do that attend upon him. And thou must have always a Silver Ring on the middle finger of the left hand held against thy face,[1] as they do yet before AMAYMON. This Great King Beleth causeth all the love that may be, both of Men and of Women, until the Master Exorcist hath had his desire fulfilled. He is of the Order of Powers, and he governeth 85 Legions of Spirits. His Noble Seal is this, which is to be worn before thee at working.

(14.) LERAJE, or LERAIKHA.—The Fourteenth Spirit is called Leraje (or Leraie). He is a Marquis Great in Power, showing himself in the likeness of an Archer clad in Green, and carrying a Bow and Quiver. He causeth all great Battles and Contests; and maketh wounds to putrefry that are made with Arrows by Archers. This belongeth unto Sagittary. He governeth 30 Legions of Spirits, and this is his Seal, etc.

(15.) ELIGOS.—The Fifteenth Spirit in Order is Eligos, a Great Duke, and appeareth in the form of a goodly Knight, carrying a Lance, an Ensign,

[1] To protect him from the flaming breath of the enraged Spirit; the design is given at the end of the instructions for the Magical Circle, etc., later on in the Goetia.

and a Serpent. He discovereth hidden things, and knoweth things to come; and of Wars, and how the Soldiers will or shall meet. He causeth the Love of Lords and Great Persons. He governeth 60 Legions of Spirits. His Seal is this, etc.

(16.) ZEPAR.—The Sixteenth Spirit is Zepar. He is a Great Duke, and appeareth in Red Apparel and Armour, like a Soldier. His office is to cause Women to love Men, and to bring them together in love. He also maketh them barren. He governeth 26 Legions of Inferior Spirits, and his Seal is this, which he obeyeth when he seeth it.

(17.) BOTIS.—The Seventeenth Spirit is Botis, a Great President, and an Earl. He appeareth at the first show in the form of an ugly Viper, then at the command of the Magician he putteth on a Human shape with Great Teeth, and two Horns, carrying a bright and sharp Sword in his hand. He telleth all things Past, and to Come, and reconcileth Friends and Foes. He ruleth over 60 Legions of Spirits, and this is his Seal, etc.

(18.) BATHIN.—The Eighteenth Spirit is Bathin. He is a Mighty and Strong Duke, and appeareth like a Strong Man with the tail of a Serpent, sitting upon a Pale-coloured [Horse?].[1] He knoweth the Virtues of Herbs and Precious Stones, and can transport men suddenly from one country to another. He ruleth over 30 Legions of Spirits. His Seal is this which is to be worn as aforesaid.

(19.) SALLOS.—The Nineteenth Spirit is Sallos (or Saleos). He is a Great and Mighty Duke, and appeareth in the form of a gallant Soldier riding on a Crocodile, with a Ducal Crown on his head, but peaceably. He causeth the Love of Women to Men, and of Men to Women; and governeth 30 Legions of Spirits. His Seal is this, etc.

(20.) PURSON.—The Twentieth Spirit is Purson, a Great King. His appearing is comely, like a Man with a Lion's face, carrying a cruel Viper in his hand, and riding upon a Bear. Going before him are many Trumpets sounding. He knoweth all things hidden, and can discover Treasure, and tell all things Past, Present, and to Come. He can take a Body either Human or Aërial, and answereth truly of all Earthly things both Secret and

---

[1] In some of the older Codices this word is left out, in others it is indistinct, but appears to be "horse," so I have put the word horse within brackets above.—TRANS. [The Quartos have "ass."—ED.]

Divine, and of the Creation of the World. He bringeth forth good Familiars, and under his Government there be 22 Legions of Spirits, partly of the Order of Virtues and partly of the Order of Thrones. His Mark, Seal, or Character is this, unto the which he oweth obedience, and which thou shalt wear in time of action, etc.

(21.) MARAX.—The Twenty-first Spirit is Marax.[1] He is a Great Earl and President. He appeareth like a great Bull with a Man's face. His office is to make Men very knowing in Astronomy, and all other Liberal Sciences; also he can give good Familiars, and wise, knowing the virtues of Herbs and Stones which be precious. He governeth 30 Legions of Spirits, and his Seal is this, which must be made and worn as aforesaid, etc.

(22.) IPOS.—The Twenty-second Spirit is Ipos. He is an Earl, and a Mighty Prince, and appeareth in the form of an Angel with a Lion's Head, and a Goose's Foot, and Hare's Tail. He knoweth all things Past, Present, and to Come. He maketh men witty and bold. He governeth 36 Legions of Spirits. His Seal is this, which thou shalt wear, etc.

(23.) AIM.—The Twenty-third Spirit is Aim. He is a Great Strong Duke. He appeareth in the form of a very handsome Man in body, but with three Heads; the first, like a Serpent, the second like a Man having two Stars on his Forehead, the third like a Calf. He rideth on a Viper, carrying a Firebrand in his Hand, wherewith he setteth cities, castles, and great Places, on fire. He maketh thee witty in all manner of ways, and giveth true answers unto private matters. He governeth 26 Legions of Inferior Spirits; and his Seal is this, which wear thou as aforesaid, etc.

(24.) NABERIUS.—The Twenty-fourth Spirit is Naberius. He is a most valiant Marquis, and showeth in the form of a Black Crane fluttering about the Circle, and when he speaketh it is with a hoarse voice. He maketh men cunning in all Arts and Sciences, but especially in the Art of Rhetoric. He restoreth lost Dignities and Honours. He governeth 19 Legions of Spirits. His Seal is this, which is to be worn, etc.

(25.) GLASYA-LABOLAS.—The Twenty-fifth Spirit is Glasya-Labolas. He is a Mighty President and Earl, and showeth himself in the form of a Dog with Wings like a Gryphon. He teacheth all Arts and Sciences in an instant, and is an Author of Bloodshed and Manslaughter. He teacheth all

---

[1] In some Codices written Morax, but I consider the above the correct orthography.

things Past, and to Come. If desired he causeth the love both of Friends and of Foes. He can make a Man to go Invisible. And he hath under his command 36 Legions of Spirits. His Seal is this, to be, etc.

(26.) BUNE, or BIMÉ.—The Twenty-sixth Spirit is Buné (or Bim). He is a Strong, Great and Mighty Duke. He appeareth in the form of a Dragon with three heads, one like a Dog, one like a Gryphon, and one like a Man. He speaketh with a high and comely Voice. He changeth the Place of the Dead, and causeth the Spirits which be under him to gather together upon your Sepulchres. He giveth Riches unto a Man, and maketh him Wise and Eloquent. He giveth true Answers unto Demands. And he governeth 30 Legions of Spirits. His Seal is this, unto the which he oweth Obedience. He hath another Seal (which is the first of these,[1] but the last is the best).[2]

(27.) RONOVÉ.—The Twenty-seventh Spirit is Ronové. He appeareth in the Form of a Monster. He teacheth the Art of Rhetoric very well, and giveth Good Servants, Knowledge of Tongues, and Favours with Friends or Foes. He is a Marquis and Great Earl; and there be under his command 19 Legions of Spirits. His Seal is this, etc.

(28.) BERITH.—The Twenty-eighth Spirit in Order, as Solomon bound them, is named Berith. He is a Mighty, Great, and Terrible Duke. He hath two other Names given unto him by men of later times, viz: BEALE, or BEAL, and BOFRY or BOLFRY. He appeareth in the Form of a Soldier with Red Clothing, riding upon a Red Horse, and having a Crown of Gold upon his head. He giveth true answers, Past, Present, and to Come.[3] Thou must make use of a Ring in calling him forth, as is before spoken of regarding Beleth.[4] He can turn all metals into Gold. He can give Dignities, and can confirm them unto Man. He speaketh with a very clear and subtle Voice. He is a Great Liar, and not to be trusted unto. He governeth 26 Legions of Spirits. His Seal is this, etc.

(29.) ASTAROTH.—The Twenty-ninth Spirit is Astaroth. He is a Mighty, Strong Duke, and appeareth in the Form of an hurtful Angel riding on an Infernal Beast like a Dragon, and carrying in his right hand a Viper. Thou must in no wise let him approach too near unto thee, lest he do thee

---

[1] Figure 30.   [2] Figure 31.
[3] This hardly agrees with the statement that he is a great liar, and not to be trusted.
[4] See *ante*, Spirit No. 13.

damage by his Noisome Breath. Wherefore the Magician must hold the Magical Ring near his face, and that will defend him. He giveth true answers of things Past, Present, and to Come, and can discover all Secrets. He will declare wittingly how the Spirits fell, if desired, and the reason of his own fall. He can make men wonderfully knowing in all Liberal Sciences. He ruleth 40 Legions of Spirits. His Seal is this, which wear thou as a Lamen before thee, or else he will not appear nor yet obey thee, etc.

(30.) FORNEUS.—The Thirtieth Spirit is Forneus. He is a Mighty and Great Marquis, and appeareth in the Form of a Great Sea-Monster. He teacheth, and maketh men wonderfully knowing in the Art of Rhetoric. He causeth men to have a Good Name, and to have the knowledge and understanding of Tongues. He maketh one to be beloved of his Foes as well as of his Friends. He governeth 29 Legions of Spirits, partly of the Order of Thrones, and partly of that of Angels. His Seal is this, which wear thou, etc.

(31.) FORAS.—The Thirty-first Spirit is Foras. He is a Mighty President, and appeareth in the Form of a Strong Man in Human Shape. He can give the understanding to Men how they may know the Virtues of all Herbs and Precious Stones. He teacheth the Arts of Logic and Ethics in all their parts. If desired he maketh men invisible,[1] and to live long, and to be eloquent. He can discover Treasures and recover things Lost. He ruleth over 29 Legions of Spirits, and his Seal is this, which wear thou, etc.

(32.) ASMODAY.—The Thirty-second Spirit is Asmoday, or Asmodai. He is a Great King, Strong, and Powerful. He appeareth with Three Heads, whereof the first is like a Bull, the second like a Man, and the third like a Ram; he hath also the tail of a Serpent, and from his mouth issue Flames of Fire. His Feet are webbed like those of a Goose. He sitteth upon an Infernal Dragon, and beareth in his hand a Lance with a Banner. He is first and choicest under the Power of AMAYMON, he goeth before all other. When the Exorcist hath a mind to call him, let it be abroad, and let him stand on his feet all the time of action, with his Cap or Head-dress off; for if it be on, AMAYMON will deceive him and call all his actions to be bewrayed.

---

[1] One or two Codices have "invincible," but "invisible" is given in the majority. Yet the form of appearance of Foras as a strong man might warrant the former, though from the nature of his offices the invincibility would probably be rather on the mental than on the physical plane.

But as soon as the Exorcist seeth Asmoday in the shape aforesaid, he shall call him by his Name, saying: "Art thou Asmoday?" and he will not deny it, and by-and-by he will bow down unto the ground. He giveth the Ring of Virtues; he teacheth the Arts of Arithmetic, Astronomy, Geometry, and all handicrafts absolutely. He giveth true and full answers unto thy demands. He maketh one Invincible. He showeth the place where Treasures lie, and guardeth it. He, amongst the Legions of AMAYMON governeth 72 Legions of Spirits Inferior. His Seal is this which thou must wear as a Lamen upon thy breast, etc.

(33.) GÄAP.—The Thirty-third Spirit is Gäap. He is a Great President and a Mighty Prince. He appeareth when the Sun is in some of the Southern Signs, in a Human Shape, going before Four Great and Mighty Kings, as if he were a Guide to conduct them along on their way. His Office is to make men Insensible or Ignorant; as also in Philosophy to make them Knowing, and in all the Liberal Sciences. He can cause Love or Hatred, also he can teach thee to consecrate those things that belong to the Dominion of AMAYMON his King. He can deliver Familiars out of the Custody of other Magicians, and answereth truly and perfectly of things Past, Present, and to Come. He can carry and re-carry men very speedily from one Kingdom to another, at the Will and Pleasure of the Exorcist. He ruleth over 66 Legions of Spirits, and he was of the Order of Potentates. His Seal is this to be made and to be worn as aforesaid, etc.

(34.) FURFUR.—The Thirty-fourth Spirit is Furfur. He is a Great and Mighty Earl, appearing in the Form of an Hart with a Fiery Tail. He never speaketh truth unless he be compelled, or brought up within a triangle, $\triangle$. Being therein, he will take upon himself the Form of an Angel. Being bidden, he speaketh with a hoarse voice. Also he will wittingly urge Love between Man and Woman. He can raise Lightnings and Thunders, Blasts, and Great Tempestuous Storms. And he giveth True Answers both of Things Secret and Divine, if commanded. He ruleth over 26 Legions of Spirits. And his Seal is this, etc.

(35.) MARCHOSIAS.—The Thirty-fifth Spirit is Marchosias. He is a Great and Mighty Marquis, appearing at first in the Form of a Wolf[1] having

---

[1] In one Codex of the seventeenth century, very badly written, it might be read "Ox" instead of "Wolf."—TRANS. [For me he appeared always like an ox, and very dazed.—ED.]

Gryphon's Wings, and a Serpent's Tail, and Vomiting Fire out of his mouth. But after a time, at the command of the Exorcist he putteth on the Shape of a Man. And he is a strong fighter. He was of the Order of Dominations. He governeth 30 Legions of Spirits. He told his Chief, who was Solomon, that after 1,200 years he had hopes to return unto the Seventh Throne. And his Seal is this, to be made and worn as a Lamen, etc.

(36.) STOLAS, or STOLOS.—The Thirty-sixth Spirit is Stolas, or Stolos. He is a Great and Powerful Prince, appearing in the Shape of a Mighty Raven at first before the Exorcist; but after he taketh the image of a Man. He teacheth the Art of Astronomy, and the Virtues of Herbs and Precious Stones. He governeth 26 Legions of Spirits; and his Seal is this, which is, etc.

(37.) PHENEX.—The Thirty-seventh Spirit is Phenex (or Pheynix). He is a Great Marquis, and appeareth like the Bird Phœnix, having the Voice of a Child. He singeth many sweet notes before the Exorcist, which he must not regard, but by-and-by he must bid him put on Human Shape. Then will he speak marvellously of all wonderful Sciences if required. He is a Poet, good and excellent. And he will be willing to perform thy requests. He hath hopes also to return to the Seventh Throne after 1,200 years more, as he said unto Solomon. He governeth 20 Legions of Spirits. And his Seal is this, which wear thou, etc.

(38.) HALPHAS, or MALTHUS.—The Thirty-eighth Spirit is Halphas, or Malthus (or Malthas). He is a Great Earl, and appeareth in the Form of a Stock-Dove. He speaketh with a hoarse Voice. His Office is to build up Towers, and to furnish them with Ammunition and Weapons, and to send Men-of-War[1] to places appointed. He ruleth over 26 Legions of Spirits, and his Seal is this, etc.[2]

(39.) MALPHAS.—The Thirty-ninth Spirit is Malphas. He appeareth at first like a Crow, but after he will put on Human Shape at the request of the Exorcist, and speak with a hoarse Voice. He is a Mighty President and Powerful. He can build Houses and High Towers, and can bring to thy Knowledge Enemies' Desires and Thoughts, and that which they have done. He giveth Good Familiars. If thou makest a Sacrifice unto him he will

---

[1] Or Warriors, or Men-at-Arms.

[2] But Malthus is certainly in heaven. See "Prometheus Unbound," Introduction by P. B. Shelley, a necromancer of note, as shown by the references in his "Hymn to Intellectual Beauty."—ED.

receive it kindly and willingly, but he will deceive him that doth it. He governeth 40 Legions of Spirits, and his Seal is this, etc.

(40.) RÄUM.—The Fortieth Spirit is Räum. He is a Great Earl; and appeareth at first in the Form of a Crow, but after the Command of the Exorcist he putteth on Human Shape. His office is to steal Treasures out King's Houses, and to carry it whither he is commanded, and to destroy Cities and Dignities of Men, and to tell all things, Past, and what Is, and what Will Be; and to cause Love between Friends and Foes. He was of the Order of Thrones. He governeth 30 Legions of Spirits; and his Seal is this, which wear thou as aforesaid.

(41.) FOCALOR.—The Forty-first Spirit is Focalor, or Forcalor, or Furcalor. He is a Mighty Duke and Strong. He appeareth in the Form of a Man with Gryphon's Wings. His office is to slay Men, and to drown them in the Waters, and to overthrow Ships of War, for he hath Power over both Winds and Seas; but he will not hurt any man or thing if he be commanded to the contrary by the Exorcist. He also hath hopes to return to the Seventh Throne after 1,000 years. He governeth 30[1] Legions of Spirits, and his Seal is this, etc.

(42.) VEPAR.—The Forty-second Spirit is Vepar, or Vephar. He is a Duke Great and Strong, and appeareth like a Mermaid. His office is to govern the Waters, and to guide Ships laden with Arms, Armour, and Ammunition, etc., thereon.[2] And at the request of the Exorcist he can cause the seas to be right stormy and to appear full of ships. Also he maketh men to die in Three Days by Putrefying Wounds or Sores, and causing Worms to breed in them. He governeth 29 Legions of Spirits, and his Seal is this, etc.

(43.) SABNOCK.—The Forty-third Spirit, as King Solomon commanded them into the Vessel of Brass, is called Sabnock, or Savnok. He is a Marquis, Mighty, Great and Strong, appearing in the Form of an Armed Soldier with a Lion's Head, riding on a pale-coloured horse. His office is to build high Towers, Castles and Cities, and to furnish them with Armour, etc. Also he can afflict Men for many days with Wounds and with Sores

---

[1] Three is given instead of 30 in several Codices; but 30 is probably the more correct.

[2] In several Codices this passage reads: "His Office is to Guide the Waters and Ships laden with Armour thereon."

rotten and full of Worms. He giveth Good Familiars at the request of the Exorcist. He commandeth 50 Legions of Spirits; and his Seal is this, etc.

(44.) SHAX.—The Forty-fourth Spirit is Shax, or Shaz (or Shass). He is a Great Marquis and appeareth in the Form of a Stock-Dove, speaking with a voice hoarse, but yet subtle. His Office is to take away the Sight, Hearing, or Understanding of any Man or Woman at the command of the Exorcist; and to steal money out of the houses of Kings, and to carry it again in 1,200 years. If commanded he will fetch Horses at the request of the Exorcist, or any other thing. But he must first be commanded into a Triangle, Δ, or else he will deceive him, and tell him many Lies. He can discover all things that are Hidden, and not kept by Wicked Spirits. He giveth good Familiars, sometimes. He governeth 30 Legions of Spirits, and his Seal is this, etc.

(45.) VINÉ.—The Forty-fifth Spirit is Viné, or Vinea. He is a Great King, and an Earl; and appeareth in the Form of a Lion,[1] riding upon a Black Horse, and bearing a Viper in his hand. His Office is to discover Things Hidden, Witches, Wizards, and Things Present, Past, and to Come. He, at the command of the Exorcist will build Towers, overthrow Great Stone Walls, and make the Waters rough with Storms. He governeth 36 Legions of Spirits. And his Seal is this, which wear thou, as aforesaid, etc.

(46.) BIFRONS.—The Forty-sixth Spirit is called Bifrons, or Bifröus, or Bifrovs. He is an Earl, and appeareth in the Form of a Monster; but after a while, at the Command of the Exorcist, he putteth on the shape of a Man. His Office is to make one knowing in Astrology, Geometry, and other Arts and Sciences. He teacheth the Virtues of Precious Stones and Woods. He changeth Dead Bodies, and putteth them in another place; also he lighteth seeming Candles upon the Graves of the Dead. He hath under his Command 6[2] Legions of Spirits. His Seal is this, which he will own and submit unto, etc.

(47.) UVALL, VUAL, or VOVAL.—The Forty-seventh Spirit is Uvall, or Vual, or Voval. He is a Duke, Great, Mighty, and Strong; and appeareth in the Form of a Mighty Dromedary at the first, but after a while at the

---

[1] Or "with the Head of a Lion," or "having a Lion's Head," in some Codices.
[2] Should probably be 60 instead of 6.

Command of the Exorcist he putteth on Human Shape, and speaketh the Egyptian Tongue, but not perfectly.[1] His Office is to procure the Love of Women, and to tell Things Past, Present, and to Come. He also procureth Friendship between Friends and Foes. He was of the Order of Potestates or Powers. He governeth 37 Legions of Spirits, and his Seal is this, to be made and worn before thee, etc.

(48.) HAAGENTI.—The Forty-eighth Spirit is Haagenti. He is a President, appearing in the Form of a Mighty Bull with Gryphon's Wings. This is at first, but after, at the Command of the Exorcist he putteth on Human Shape. His Office is to make Men wise, and to instruct them in divers things; also to Transmute all Metals into Gold; and to change Wine into Water, and Water into Wine. He governeth 33 Legions of Spirits, and his Seal is this, etc.

(49.) CROCELL.—The Forty-ninth Spirit is Crocell, or Crokel. He appeareth in the Form of an Angel. He is a Duke Great and Strong, speaking something Mystically of Hidden Things. He teacheth the Art of Geometry and the Liberal Sciences. He, at the Command of the Exorcist, will produce Great Noises like the Rushings of many Waters, although there be none. He warmeth Waters, and discovereth Baths. He was of the Order of Potestates, or Powers, before his fall, as he declared unto the King Solomon. He governeth 48 Legions of Spirits. His Seal is this, the which wear thou as aforesaid.

(50.) FURCAS.—The Fiftieth Spirit is Furcas. He is a Knight, and appeareth in the Form of a Cruel Old Man with a long Beard and a hoary Head, riding upon a pale-coloured Horse, with a Sharp Weapon in his hand. His Office is to teach the Arts of Philosophy, Astrology, Rhetoric, Logic, Cheiromancy, and Pyromancy, in all their parts, and perfectly. He hath under his Power 20 Legions of Spirits. His Seal, or Mark, is thus made, etc.

(51.) BALAM.—The Fifty-first Spirit is Balam or Balaam. He is a Terrible, Great, and Powerful King. He appeareth with three Heads: the first is like that of a Bull; the second is like that of a Man; the third is like that of a Ram. He hath the Tail of a Serpent, and Flaming Eyes. He rideth upon a furious Bear, and carrieth a Goshawk upon his Fist. He

---

[1] He can nowadays converse in sound though colloquial Coptic.—ED.

speaketh with a hoarse Voice, giving True Answers of Things Past, Present, and to Come. He maketh men to go Invisible, and also to be Witty. He governeth 40 Legions of Spirits. His Seal is this, etc.

(52.) ALLOCES.—The Fifty-second Spirit is Alloces, or Alocas. He is a Duke, Great, Mighty, and Strong, appearing in the Form of a Soldier[1] riding upon a Great Horse. His Face is like that of a Lion, very Red, and having Flaming Eyes. His Speech is hoarse and very big.[2] His Office is to teach the Art of Astronomy, and all the Liberal Sciences. He bringeth unto thee Good Familiars; also he ruleth over 36 Legions of Spirits. His Seal is this, which, etc.

(53.) CAMIO or CAÏM.—The Fifty-third Spirit is Camio, or Caïm. He is a Great President, and appeareth in the Form of the Bird called a Thrush at first, but afterwards he putteth on the Shape of a Man carrying in his Hand a Sharp Sword. He seemeth to answer in Burning Ashes, or in Coals of Fire. He is a Good Disputer. His Office is to give unto Men the Understanding of all Birds, Lowing of Bullocks, Barking of Dogs, and other Creatures; and also of the Voice of the Waters. He giveth True Answers of Things to Come. He was of the Order of Angels, but now ruleth over 30 Legions of Spirits Infernal. His Seal is this, which wear thou, etc.

(54.) MURMUR, or MURMUS.—The Fifty-fourth Spirit is called Murmur, or Murmus, or Murmux. He is a Great Duke, and an Earl; and appeareth in the Form of a Warrior riding upon a Gryphon, with a Ducal Crown upon his Head. There do go before him those his Ministers with great Trumpets sounding. His Office is to teach Philosophy perfectly, and to constrain Souls Deceased to come before the Exorcist to answer those questions which he may wish to put to them, if desired. He was partly of the Order of Thrones, and partly of that of Angels. He now ruleth 30 Legions of Spirits. And his Seal is this, etc.

(55.) OROBAS.—The Fifty-fifth Spirit is Orobas. He is a Great and Mighty Prince, appearing at first like a Horse; but after the command of the Exorcist he putteth on the Image of a Man. His Office is to discover all things Past, Present, and to Come; also to give Dignities, and Prelacies, and the Favour of Friends and of Foes. He giveth True Answers of Divinity, and of the Creation of the World. He is very faithful unto the Exorcist, and will not

---

[1] Or Warrior.   [2] Thus expressed in the Codices.

suffer him to be tempted of any Spirit. He governeth 20 Legions of Spirits. His Seal is this, etc.

(56.) GREMORY, or GAMORI.—The Fifty-sixth Spirit is Gremory, or Gamori. He is a Duke Strong and Powerful, and appeareth in the Form of a Beautiful Woman, with a Duchess's Crown tied about her waist, and riding on a Great Camel. His Office is to tell of all Things Past, Present, and to Come; and of Treasures Hid, and what they lie in; and to procure the Love of Women both Young and Old. He governeth 26 Legions of Spirits, and his Seal is this, etc.

(57.) OSÉ, or VOSO.—The Fifty-seventh Spirit is Oso, Osé, or Voso. He is a Great President, and appeareth like a Leopard at the first, but after a little time he putteth on the Shape of a Man. His Office is to make one cunning in the Liberal Sciences, and to give True Answers of Divine and Secret Things; also to change a Man into any Shape that the Exorcist pleaseth, so that he that is so changed will not think any other thing than that he is in verity that Creature or Thing he is changed into. He governeth 3[1] Legions of Spirits, and this is his Seal, etc.

(58.) AMY, or AVNAS.—The Fifty-eighth Spirit is Amy, or Avnas. He is a Great President, and appeareth at first in the Form of a Flaming Fire; but after a while he putteth on the Shape of a Man. His office is to make one Wonderful Knowing[2] in Astrology and all the Liberal Sciences. He giveth Good Familiars, and can bewray Treasure that is kept by Spirits. He governeth 36 Legions of Spirits, and his Seal is this, etc.

(59.) ORIAX, or ORIAS.—The Fifty-ninth Spirit is Oriax, or Orias. He is a Great Marquis, and appeareth in the Form of a Lion,[3] riding upon a Horse Mighty and Strong, with a Serpent's Tail;[4] and he holdeth in his Right Hand two Great Serpents hissing. His Office is to teach the Virtues of the Stars, and to know the Mansions of the Planets, and how to understand their Virtues. He also transformeth Men, and he giveth Dignities, Prelacies, and Confirmation thereof; also Favour with Friends and with Foes. He doth govern 30 Legions of Spirits; and his Seal is this, etc.

---

[1] Should probably be 30. For these 72 Great Spirits of the Book Goetia are all Princes and Leaders of numbers.

[2] Thus in the actual Text.

[3] Or "with the Face of a Lion."

[4] The horse, or the Markis?—ED.

(60.) VAPULA, or NAPHULA.—The Sixtieth Spirit is Vapula, or Naphula. He is a Duke Great, Mighty, and Strong; appearing in the Form of a Lion with Gryphon's Wings. His Office is to make Men Knowing in all Handicrafts and Professions, also in Philosophy, and other Sciences. He governeth 36 Legions of Spirits, and his Seal or Character is thus made, and thou shalt wear it as aforesaid, etc.

(61.) ZAGAN.—The Sixty-first Spirit is Zagan. He is a Great King and President, appearing at first in the Form of a Bull with Gryphon's Wings; but after a while he putteth on Human Shape. He maketh Men Witty. He can turn Wine into Water, and Blood into Wine, also Water into Wine. He can turn all Metals into Coin of the Dominion that Metal is of. He can even make Fools Wise. He governeth 33 Legions of Spirits, and his Seal is this, etc.

(62.) VOLAC, or VALAK, or VALU, or UALAC.—The Sixty-second Spirit is Volac, or Valak, or Valu. He is a President Mighty and Great, and appeareth like a Child with Angel's Wings, riding on a Two-headed Dragon. His Office is to give True Answers of Hidden Treasures, and to tell where Serpents may be seen. The which he will bring unto the Exorciser without any Force or Strength being by him employed. He governeth 38 Legions of Spirits, and his Seal is thus.

(63.) ANDRAS.—The Sixty-third Spirit is Andras. He is a Great Marquis, appearing in the Form of an Angel with a Head like a Black Night Raven, riding upon a strong Black Wolf, and having a Sharp and Bright Sword flourished aloft in his hand. His Office is to sow Discords. If the Exorcist have not a care, he will slay both him and his fellows. He governeth 30 Legions of Spirits, and this is his Seal, etc.

(64.) HAURES, or HAURAS, or HAVRES, or FLAUROS.—The Sixty-fourth Spirit is Haures, or Hauras, or Havres, or Flauros. He is a Great Duke, and appeareth at first like a Leopard, Mighty, Terrible, and Strong, but after a while, at the Command of the Exorcist, he putteth on Human Shape with Eyes Flaming and Fiery, and a most Terrible Countenance. He giveth True Answers of all things, Present, Past, and to Come. But if he be not commanded into a Triangle, △, he will Lie in all these Things, and deceive and beguile the Exorcist in these things or in such and such business. He will, lastly, talk of the Creation of the World, and of Divinity, and of how he and other Spirits fell. He destroyeth and burneth up those who be the Enemies of the Exorcist should he so desire it; also he will not suffer him to be tempted by any other Spirit or otherwise. He governeth 36 Legions of Spirits, and his Seal is this, to be worn as a Lamen, etc.

(65.) ANDREALPHUS.—The Sixty-fifth Spirit is Andrealphus. He is a Mighty Marquis, appearing at first in the form of a Peacock, with great Noises. But after a time he putteth on Human shape. He can teach Geometry perfectly. He maketh Men very subtle therein; and in all Things pertaining unto Mensuration or Astronomy. He can transform a Man into the Likeness of a Bird. He governeth 30 Legions of Infernal Spirits, and his Seal is this, etc.

(66.) CIMEJES, or CIMEIES, or KIMARIS.—The Sixty-sixth Spirit is Cimejes, or Cimeies, or Kimaris. He is a Marquis, Mighty, Great, Strong and Powerful, appearing like a Valiant Warrior riding upon a goodly Black Horse. He ruleth over all Spirits in the parts of Africa. His Office is to teach perfectly Grammar, Logic, Rhetoric, and to discover things Lost or Hidden, and Treasures. He governeth 20 Legions of Infernals; and his Seal is this, etc.

(67.) AMDUSIAS, or AMDUKIAS.—The Sixty-seventh Spirit is Amdusias, or Amdukias. He is a Duke Great and Strong, appearing at first like a Unicorn, but at the request of the Exorcist he standeth before him in Human Shape, causing Trumpets, and all manner of Musical Instruments to be heard, but not soon or immediately. Also he can cause Trees to bend and incline according to the Exorcist's Will. He giveth Excellent Familiars. He governeth 29 Legions of Spirits. And his Seal is this, etc.

(68.) BELIAL.—The Sixty-eighth Spirit is Belial. He is a Mighty and a Powerful King, and was created next after LUCIFER. He appeareth in the Form of Two Beautiful Angels sitting in a Chariot of Fire. He speaketh with a Comely Voice, and declareth that he fell first from among the worthier sort, that were before Michael, and other Heavenly Angels. His Office is to distribute Presentations and Senatorships, etc., and to cause favour of Friends and of Foes. He giveth excellent Familiars, and governeth 80[1] Legions of Spirits. Note well that this King Belial must have Offerings, Sacrifices and Gifts presented unto him by the Exorcist, or else he will not

[1] Perhaps an error for 30.—TRANS. The actual number is 50; at least it was in 1898.—ED.

give True Answers unto his Demands. But then he tarrieth not one hour in the Truth, unless he be constrained by Divine Power. And his Seal is this, which is to be worn as aforesaid, etc.

(69.) DECARABIA.—The Sixty-ninth Spirit is Decarabia. He appeareth in the Form of a Star in a Pentacle, ✦, at first; but after, at the command of the Exorcist, he putteth on the Image of a Man. His Office is to discover the Virtues of Birds and Precious Stones, and to make the Similitude of all kinds of Birds to fly before the Exorcist, singing and drinking as natural Birds do. He governeth 30 Legions of Spirits, being himself a Great Marquis. And this is his Seal, which is to be worn, etc.

(70.) SEERE, SEAR, or SEIR.—The Seventieth Spirit is Seere, Sear, or Seir. He is a Mighty Prince, and Powerful, under AMAYMON, King of the East. He appeareth in the Form of a Beautiful Man, riding upon a Winged Horse. His Office is to go and come; and to bring abundance of things to pass on a sudden, and to carry or re-carry anything whither thou wouldest have it to go, or whence thou wouldest have it from. He can pass over the whole Earth in the twinkling of an Eye. He giveth a True relation of all sorts of Theft, and of Treasure hid, and of many other things. He is of an indifferent Good Nature, and is willing to do anything which the Exorcist desireth. He governeth 26 Legions of Spirits. And this his Seal is to be worn, etc.

(71.) DANTALION.—The Seventy-first Spirit is Dantalion. He is a Duke Great and Mighty, appearing in the Form of a Man with many Countenances, all Men's and Women's Faces; and he hath a Book in his right hand. His Office is to teach all Arts and Sciences unto any; and to declare the Secret Counsels of any one; for he knoweth the Thoughts of all Men and Women, and can change them at his Will. He can cause Love, and show the Similitude of any person, and show the same by a Vision, let them be in what part of the World they Will. He governeth 36 Legions of Spirits; and this is his Seal, which wear thou, etc.

(72.) ANDROMALIUS.—The Seventy-second Spirit in Order is named Andromalius. He is an Earl, Great and Mighty, appearing in the Form of a Man holding a Great Serpent in his Hand. His Office is to bring back both a Thief, and the Goods which be stolen; and to discover all Wickedness, and Underhand Dealing; and to punish all Thieves and other Wicked

People; and also to discover Treasures that be Hid. He ruleth over 36 Legions of Spirits. His Seal is this, the which wear thou as aforesaid, etc.

THESE be the 72 Mighty Kings and Princes which King Solomon Commanded into a Vessel of Brass, together with their Legions. Of whom BELIAL, BILETH, ASMODAY, and GAAP, were Chief. And it is to be noted that Solomon did this because of their pride, for he never declared other reason why he thus bound them. And when he had thus bound them up and sealed the Vessel, he by Divine Power did chase them all into a deep Lake or Hole in Babylon. And they of Babylon, wondering to see such a thing, they did then go wholly into the Lake, to break the Vessel open, expecting to find great store of Treasure therein. But when they had broken it open, out flew the Chief Spirits immediately, with their Legions following them; and they were all restored to their former places except BELIAL, who entered into a certain Image, and thence gave answers unto those who did offer Sacrifices unto him, and did worship the Image as their God, etc.

OBSERVATIONS.

FIRST, thou shalt know and observe the Moon's Age for thy working. The best days be when the Moon Luna is 2, 4, 6, 8, 10, 12, or 14 days old, as Solomon saith; and no other days be profitable. The Seals of the 72 Kings are to be made in Metals. The Chief Kings' in Sol (Gold); Marquises' in Luna (Silver); Dukes' in Venus (Copper); Prelacies' in Jupiter (Tin); Knights' in Saturn (Lead); Presidents' in Mercury (Mercury); Earls' in Venus (Copper), and Luna (Silver), alike equal, etc.

THESE 72 Kings be under the Power of AMAYMON, CORSON, ZIMIMAY or ZIMINIAR, and GÖAP, who are the Four Great Kings ruling in the Four Quarters, or Cardinal Points,[1] viz.: East, West, North, and South, and are not to be called forth except it be upon Great Occasions; but are to be Invocated and Commanded to send such or such a Spirit that is under their

---

[1] These four Great Kings are usually called Oriens, or Uriens, Paymon or Paymonia, Ariton or Egyn, and Amaymon or Amaimon. By the Rabbins they are frequently entitled: Samael, Azazel, Azäel, and Mahazael.

Power and Rule, as is shown in the following Invocations or Conjurations. And the Chief Kings may be bound from 9 till 12 o'clock at Noon, and from 3 till sunset; Marquises may be bound from 3 in the afternoon till 9 at Night, and from 9 at Night till Sunrise; Dukes may be bound from Sunrise till Noonday in Clear Weather; Prelates may be bound any hour of the Day; Knights may from Dawning of Day till Sunrise, or from 4 o'clock till Sunset; Presidents may be bound at any time, excepting Twilight, at Night, unless the King whom they are under be Invocated; and Counties or Earls any hour of the Day, so it be in Woods, or in any other places whither men resort not, or where no noise is, etc.

CLASSIFIED LIST OF THE 72 CHIEF SPIRITS OF THE GOETIA, ACCORDING TO RESPECTIVE RANK.

(Seal in Gold.) KINGS: (1.) Bael; (9.) Paimon; (13.) Beleth; (20.) Purson; (32.) Asmoday; (45.) Viné; (51.) Balam; (61.) Zagan; (68.) Belial.

(Seal in Copper.) DUKES.—(2.) Agares; (6.) Valefor; (8.) Barbatos; (11.) Gusion; (15.) Eligos; (16.) Zepar; (18.) Bathin; (19.) Sallos; (23.) Aim; (26.) Buné; (28.) Berith; (29.) Astaroth; (41.) Focalor; (42.) Vepar; (47.) Vual; (49.) Crocell; (52.) Alloces; (54.) Murmur; (56.) Gremory; (60.) Vapula; (64.) Haures; (67.) Amdusias; (71.) Dantalion.

(Seal in Tin.) PRINCES and PRELATES.—(3.) Vassago; (12.) Sitri; (22.) Ipos; (33.) Gäap; (36.) Stolas; (55.) Orobas; (70.) Seere.

(Seal in Silver.) MARQUISES.—(4.) Samigina; (7.) Amon; (14.) Lerajé; (24.) Naberius; (27.) Ronové; (30.) Forneus; (35.) Marchosias; (37.) Phenex; (43.) Sabnock; (44.) Shax; (59.) Orias; (63.) Andras; (65.) Andrealphus; (66) Cimeies; (69.) Decarabia.

(Seal in Mercury.) PRESIDENTS.—(5.) Marbas; (10.) Buer; (17.) Botis; (21.) Marax; (25.) Glasya-Labolas; (31.) Foras; (33.) Gäap; (39.) Malphas; (48.) Häagenti; (53.) Caïm; (57.) Ose; (58.) Amy; (61.) Zagan; (62.) Valac.

(Seal in Copper and Silver alike equal.) EARLS, or COUNTS.—(17.)

Botis; (21.) Marax; (25.) Glasya-Labolas; (27.) Ronové; (34.) Furfur; (38.) Halphas; (40.) Räum; (45.) Viné; (46.) Bifrons; (72.) Andromalius. (Seal in Lead.) KNIGHTS.—(50.) Furcas.

NOTE.—It will be remarked that several among the above Spirits possess two titles of different ranks: *e.g.*, (45.) Viné is both King and Earl; (25.) Glasya-Labolas is both President and Earl, etc. " Prince " and " Prelate " are apparently used as interchangeable terms. Probably the Seals of Earls should be made in Iron, and those of Presidents in mixture either of Copper and Silver, or of Silver and Mercury; as otherwise the Metal of one Planet, Mars, is excluded from the List; the Metals attributed to the Seven Planets being: to Saturn, Lead; to Jupiter, Tin; to Mars, Iron; to the Sun, Gold; to Venus, Copper; to Mercury, Mercury and mixtures of Metals, and to Luna, Silver.

In a manuscript codex by Dr. Rudd, which is in the British Museum, Hebrew names of these 72 Spirits are given; but it appears to me that many are manifestly incorrect in orthography. The codex in question, though beautifully written, also contains many other errors, particularly in the Sigils. Such as they are, these names in the Hebrew of Dr. Rudd are here shown. (*See Figures* 81 *to* 152 *inclusive.*)

THE MAGICAL CIRCLE.

THIS is the Form of the Magical Circle of King Solomon, the which he made that he might preserve himself therein from the malice of these Evil Spirits. (*See Frontispiece, Figure* 153.) This Magical Circle is to be made 9 feet across, and the Divine Names are to be written round it, beginning at EHYEH, and ending at LEVANAH, Luna.

(Colours.—The space between the outer and inner circles, where the serpent is coiled, with the Hebrew names written along his body, is bright deep yellow. The square in the centre of the circle, where the word "Master" is written, is filled in with red. All names and letters are in black. In the Hexagrams the outer triangles where the letters A, D, O, N, A, I, appear are filled in with bright yellow, the centres, where the T-shaped crosses are, blue or green. In the Pentagrams outside the circle, the outer triangles where "Te, tra, gram, ma, ton," is written are filled in bright yellow, and the centres with the T crosses written therein are red.[1])

---

[1] The coiled serpent is only shown in one private codex, the Hebrew names being in most cases simply written round in a somewhat spiral arrangement within the double circle. It is to be remembered that Hebrew is always written from right to left, instead of from left to right like ordinary European languages. The small Maltese crosses are placed to mark the conclusion of each separate set of Hebrew names. These names are those of Deity Angels and Archangels allotted by the Qabalists to each of the 9 first Sephiroth or Divine Emanations. In English letters they run thus, beginning from the head of the serpent: + Ehyeh Kether Metatron Chaioth Ha-Qadesh Rashith Ha-Galgalim S.P.M. (for "Sphere of the Primum Mobile") + Iah Chokmah Ratziel Auphanim Masloth S.S.F. (for "Sphere of the Fixed Stars," or S.Z. for "Sphere of the Zodiac") + Iehovah Elohim Binah Tzaphquiel Aralim Shabbathai S. (for "Sphere") of Saturn + El Chesed Tzadquiel Chaschmalim Tzedeq S. of Jupiter + Elohim Gibor Geburah Kamael Seraphim Madim S. of Mars + Iehovah Eloah Va-Daäth Tiphereth Rapha-

THE MAGICAL TRIANGLE OF SOLOMON.

THIS is the Form of the Magical Triangle, into the which Solomon did command the Evil Spirits. It is to be made at 2 feet distance from the Magical Circle and it is 3 feet across. (*See Frontispiece Figure* 154.) Note that this triangle is to be placed toward that quarter whereunto the Spirit belongeth. And the base of the triangle is to be nearest unto the Circle, the apex pointing in the direction of the quarter of the Spirit. Observe thou also the Moon in thy working, as aforesaid, etc. Anaphaxeton is sometimes written Anepheneton.

(Colours.—Triangle outlined in black; name of Michael black on white ground; the three Names without the triangle written in red; circle in centre entirely filled in in dark green.)

THE HEXAGRAM OF SOLOMON.

THIS is the Form of the Hexagram of Solomon, the figure whereof is to be made on parchment of a calf's skin, and worn at the skirt of thy white vestment, and covered with a cloth of fine linen white and pure, the which is to be shown unto the Spirits when they do appear, so that they be compelled to take human shape upon them and be obedient.

(Colours.—Circle, Hexagram, and T cross in centre outlined in black, Maltese crosses black; the five exterior triangles of the Hexagram where Te, tra, gram, ma, ton, is written, are filled in with bright yellow; the T cross in centre is red, with the three little squares therein in black. The lower exterior triangle, where the Sigil is drawn in black, is left white. The words "Tetragrammaton" and "Tau" are in black letters; and AGLA with Alpha and Omega in red letters.)

THE PENTAGRAM OF SOLOMON.

THIS is the Form of the Pentagram of Solomon, the figure whereof is to be made in Sol or Luna (Gold or Silver), and worn upon thy breast; having

ël Malakim Shemesh S. of the Sun + Iehovah Tzabaoth Netzach Haniel Elohim Nogah S. of Venus. + Elohim Tzabaoth Hod Michaël Beni Elohim Kokav S. of Mercury + Shaddaï El Chai Iesod Gabriel Cherubim Levanah S. of the Moon +.

the Seal of the Spirit required upon the other side thereof. It is to preserve thee from danger, and also to command the Spirits by.

(Colours.—Circle and pentagram outlined in black. Names and Sigils within Pentagram black also. "Tetragrammaton" in red letters. Ground of centre of Pentagram, where "Soluzen" is written, green. External angles of Pentagram where "Abdia," "Ballaton," "Halliza," etc., are written, blue.)

THE MAGIC RING OR DISC OF SOLOMON.

THIS is the Form of the Magic Ring, or rather Disc, of Solomon, the figure whereof is to be made in gold or silver. It is to be held before the face of the exorcist to preserve him from the stinking sulphurous fumes and flaming breath of the Evil Spirits.

(Colour.—Bright yellow. Letters, black.)

THE VESSEL OF BRASS.

THIS is the Form of the Vessel of Brass wherein King Solomon did shut up the Evil Spirits, etc. (*See Figures* 158 *and* 159.) (Somewhat different forms are given in the various codices. The seal in Figure 160 was made in brass to cover this vessel with at the top. This history of the genii shut up in the brazen vessel by King Solomon recalls the story of "The Fisherman and the Jinni" in "The Arabian Nights." In this tale, however, there was only one jinni shut up in a vessel of yellow brass the which was covered at the top with a leaden seal. This jinni tells the fisherman that his name is Sakhr, or Sacar.)

(Colour.—Bronze. Letters.—Black on a red band.)

THE SECRET SEAL OF SOLOMON.

THIS is the Form of the Secret Seal of Solomon, wherewith he did bind and seal up the aforesaid Spirits with their legions in the Vessel of Brass.

This seal is to be made by one that is clean both inwardly and outwardly, and that hath not defiled himself by any woman in the space of a month, but hath in prayer and fasting desired of God to forgive him all his sins, etc.

It is to be made on the day of Mars or Saturn (Tuesday or Saturday) at night at 12 o'clock, and written upon virgin parchment with the blood of a black cock that never trode hen. Note that on this night the moon must be increasing in light (*i.e.* going from new to full) and in the Zodiacal Sign of Virgo. And when the seal is so made thou shalt perfume it with alum, raisins dried in the sun, dates, cedar, and lignum aloes.

Also by this seal King Solomon did command all the aforesaid Spirits into the Vessel of Brass, and did seal it up with this same seal. He by it gained the love of all manner of persons, and overcame in battle, for neither weapons, nor fire, nor water could hurt him. And this privy seal was made to cover the vessel at the top withal, etc.

Note: Figures 162 to 174 inclusive are interesting as showing a marked resemblance to the central design of the Secret Seal. It will be observed that the evident desire is to represent hieroglyphically a person raising his or her hands in adoration. Nearly all are stone sepulchral steles, and the execution of them is rough and primitive in the extreme. Most are in the Musée du Louvre at Paris.

Figures 162 and 163 are from the district of Constantine and show a figure raising its arms in adoration.

In Figure 164, also from Constantine, the person bears a palm branch in the right hand. Above is a hieroglyphic representing either the Lunar Disc or the Sun in the heavens; but more probably the former.

Figure 165 is a more complicated stele. Above is the symbol already mentioned, then comes the sign of the Pentagram, represented by a five-pointed star, towards which the person raises his or her hands. Besides the latter is a rude form of caduceus. A brief inscription follows in the Punic character. The Punic or Carthaginian language is usually considered to have been a dialect of Phœnician, and Carthage was of course a colony of Tyre. Beneath the Punic inscription is a horse's head in better drawing than the sculpture of the rest of the stele, which would seem to imply that the rudeness of the representation of the human figure is intentional. This and the following stele are also from Constantine.

In Figure 166 again, the horse is best delineated by far. In addition to the other symbols there is either a hand or a foot, for it is almost impossible to distinguish which, at the head of the stele, followed by an egg-and-tongue moulding. The figure of the person with the arms raised is treated as a pure hieroglyphic and is placed between two rude caducei. The Lunar or Solar symbol follows.

Figure 167, also from Constantine, shows the last-mentioned symbol above. The figure with the arms raised is simply a hieroglyph, and is placed between an arm and hand on the one side, and a rude caduceus on the other.

Figure 168 shows the person holding a rude caduceus in the right hand, and standing above a dolphin. This latter, as in the case of the horse in 165 and 166, is by far the best delineated.

Figure 169, this also being from Constantine, shows the usual human hieroglyph between a caduceus and a crescent.

Figure 170 is from the site of ancient Carthage. It is very rough in workmanship, and the designs are mere scratchings on the stone. The *ensemble* has the effect of an evil Sigil.

Figure 171 is also from Carthage and the various symbols appear to have become compressed into and synthesised in the form of a peculiarly evil-looking caduceus.

Figure 172 is from the decoration of a sepulchral urn found at Oldenburgh in Germany. It is remarkable as showing the same hieroglyphic human form with the crescent above; the latter in the Secret Seal of Solomon has a flattened top, and is therefore more like a bowl, and is placed across the hieroglyph.

Figure 173 is an Egyptian design which would show an analogy between the symbol and the idea of the force of the creation.

Figure 174 is a stele from Phœnicia somewhat similar to the others, except that the rudimentary caducei in Figures 166 and 170 are here replaced by two roughly drawn Ionic columns.

These last three designs are taken from the work of the Chevalier Emile Soldi-Colbert de Beaulieu, on the "*Langue Sacrée.*"

In Figure 175 is given the Seal of the Spirit HALAHEL. This Spirit is said to be under the rule of BAEL, and to be of a mixed nature, partly good and partly evil, like the spirits of Theurgia-Goetia which follow in the second book of the Lemegeton.

NOTE.—I am not responsible for the accuracy of the above note.—ED.

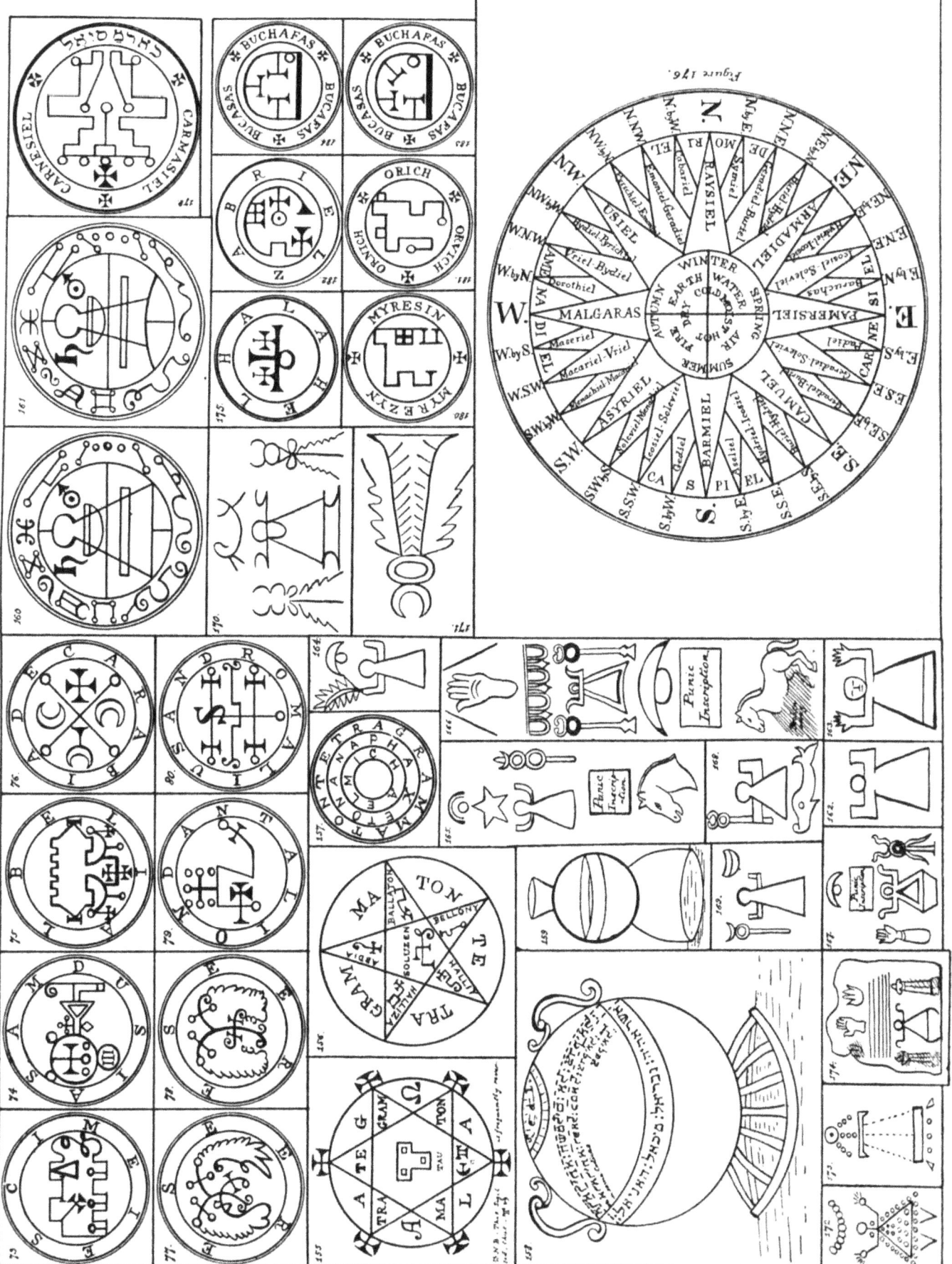

THE OTHER MAGICAL REQUISITES.

THE other magical requisites are: a sceptre, a sword, a mitre, a cap, a long white robe of linen, and other garments for the purpose;[1] also a girdle of lion's skin three inches broad, with all the names written about it which be round the outmost part of the Magical Circle. Also perfumes, and a chafing-dish of charcoal kindled to put the fumes on, to smoke or perfume the place appointed for action; also anointing oil to anoint thy temples and thine eyes with; and fair water to wash thyself in. And in so doing, thou shalt say as David said:

THE ADORATION AT THE BATH.

"THOU shalt purge me with hyssop, O Lord! and I shall be clean: Thou shalt wash me, and I shall be whiter than snow."

And at the putting on of thy garments thou shalt say:

THE ADORATION AT THE INDUING OF THE VESTMENTS.

"BY the figurative mystery of these holy vestures (or of this holy vestment) I will clothe me with the armour of salvation in the strength of the Most High, ANCOR; AMACOR; AMIDES; THEODONIAS; ANITOR; that my desired end may be effected through Thy strength, O ADONAI! unto Whom the praise and glory will for ever and ever belong! Amen!"

After thou hast so done, make prayers unto God according unto thy work, as Solomon hath commanded.

THE CONJURATION TO CALL FORTH ANY OF THE AFORESAID SPIRITS.

I DO invoke and conjure thee, O Spirit, N.[2]; and being with power armed from the SUPREME MAJESTY, I do strongly command thee, by BERALANENSIS, BALDACHIENSIS, PAUMACHIA, and APOLOGIÆ SEDES; by the most Powerful Princes, Genii, Liachidæ, and Ministers of the Tartarean

---

[1] In many codices it is written "a sceptre or sword, a mitre or cap." By the "other garments" would be meant not only under-garments, but also mantles of different colours.

[2] Here interpolate the name of the Spirit desired to be invocated. In some of the codices there are faint variations in the form of wording of the conjurations, but not sufficient to change the sense, *e.g.*, "Tartarean abode" for "Tartarean seat," etc.

Abode; and by the Chief Prince of the Seat of Apologia in the Ninth Legion, I do invoke thee, and by invocating conjure thee. And being armed with power from the SUPREME MAJESTY, I do strongly command thee, by Him Who spake and it was done, and unto whom all creatures be obedient. Also I, being made after the image of GOD, endued with power from GOD, and created according unto His will, do exorcise thee by that most mighty and powerful name of GOD, EL, strong and wonderful; O thou Spirit N. And I command thee by Him who spake the Word and His FIAT was accomplished, and by all the names of GOD. Also by the names ADONAI, EL, ELOHIM, ELOHI, EHYEH ASHER EHYEH, ZABAOTH, ELION, IAH, TETRAGRAMMATON, SHADDÄI, LORD GOD MOST HIGH, I do exorcise thee and do powerfully command thee, O thou spirit N., that thou dost forthwith appear unto me here before this Circle in a fair human shape, without any deformity or tortuosity. And by this ineffable name, TETRAGRAMMATON IEHOVAH, do I command thee, at the which being heard the elements are overthrown, the air is shaken, the sea runneth back, the fire is quenched, the earth trembleth, and all the hosts of the celestials, terrestrials, and infernals do tremble together, and are troubled and confounded. Wherefore come thou, O Spirit N., forthwith, and without delay, from any or all parts of the world wherever thou mayest be, and make rational answers unto all things that I shall demand of thee. Come thou peaceably, visibly, and affably, now, and without delay, manifesting that which I shall desire. For thou art conjured by the name of the LIVING and TRUE GOD, HELIOREN, wherefore fulfil thou my commands, and persist thou therein unto the end, and according unto mine interest, visibly and affably speaking unto me with a voice clear and intelligible without any ambiguity.

REPEAT this conjuration as often as thou pleasest, and if the Spirit come not yet, say as followeth:

THE SECOND CONJURATION.

I DO invocate, conjure, and command thee, O thou Spirit N., to appear and to show thyself visibly unto me before this Circle in fair and comely shape, without any deformity or tortuosity; by the name and in the name IAH and VAU, which Adam heard and spake; and by the name of GOD, AGLA, which

Lot heard and was saved with his family; and by the name IOTH, which Iacob heard from the angel wrestling with him, and was delivered from the hand of Esau his brother; and by the name ANAPHAXETON[1] which Aaron heard and spake and was made wise; and by the name ZABAOTH,[2] which Moses named and all the rivers were turned into blood; and by the name ASHER EHYEH ORISTON, which Moses named, and all the rivers brought forth frogs, and they ascended into the houses, destroying all things; and by the name ELION, which Moses named, and there was great hail such as had not been since the beginning of the world; and by the name ADONAI, which Moses named, and there came up locusts, which appeared upon the whole land, and devoured all which the hail had left; and by the name SCHEMA AMATHIA which Ioshua called upon, and the sun stayed his course; and by the name ALPHA and OMEGA, which Daniel named, and destroyed Bel, and slew the Dragon; and in the name EMMANUEL, which the three children, Shadrach, Meshach and Abed-nego, sang in the midst of the fiery furnace, and were delivered; and by the name HAGIOS; and by the SEAL[3] OF ADONAI; and by ISCHYROS, ATHANATOS, PARACLETOS; and by O THEOS, ICTROS, ATHANATOS; and by these three secret names, AGLA, ON, TETRAGRAMMATON, do I adjure and constrain thee. And by these names, and by all the other names of the LIVING and TRUE GOD, the LORD ALMIGHTY, I do exorcise and command thee, O Spirit N., even by Him Who spake the Word and it was done, and to Whom all creatures are obedient; and by the dreadful judgments of GOD; and by the uncertain Sea of Glass, which is before the DIVINE MAJESTY, mighty and powerful; by the four beasts before the throne, having eyes before and behind; by the fire round about the throne; by the holy angels of Heaven; and by the mighty wisdom of GOD; I do potently exorcise thee, that thou appearest here before this Circle, to fulfil my will in all things which shall seem good unto me; by the Seal of BASDATHEA BALDACHIA; and by this name PRIMEUMATON, which Moses named, and the earth opened, and did swallow up Kora, Dathan, and Abiram. Wherefore thou shalt make faithful answers unto all my demands,

---

[1] Or "Anapezeton."

[2] Or "Tzabaoth."

[3] In some "By the Seat of Adonai" or "By the Throne of Adonai." In these conjurations and elsewhere in the body of the text I have given the divine names as correctly as possible.

O Spirit N., and shalt perform all my desires so far as in thine office thou art capable hereof. Wherefore, come thou, visibly, peaceably, and affably, now without delay, to manifest that which I desire, speaking with a clear and perfect voice, intelligibly, and to mine understanding.

IF HE come not yet at the rehearsal of these two first conjurations (but without doubt he will), say on as followeth; it being a constraint:

THE CONSTRAINT.

I DO conjure thee, O thou Spirit N., by all the most glorious and efficacious names of the MOST GREAT AND INCOMPREHENSIBLE LORD GOD OF HOSTS, that thou comest quickly and without delay from all parts and places of the earth and world wherever thou mayest be, to make rational answers unto my demands, and that visibly and affably, speaking with a voice intelligible unto mine understanding as aforesaid. I conjure and constrain thee, O thou Spirit N., by all the names aforesaid; and in addition by these seven great names wherewith Solomon the Wise bound thee and thy companions in a Vessel of Brass, ADONAI, PREYAI or PRERAI, TETRAGRAMMATON, ANAPHAXETON or ANEPHENETON, INESSENFATOAL or INESSENFATALL, PATHTUMON or PATHATUMON, and ITEMON; that thou appearest here before this Circle to fulfil my will in all things that seem good unto me. And if thou be still so disobedient, and refusest still to come, I will in the power and by the power of the name of the SUPREME AND EVERLASTING LORD GOD Who created both thee and me and all the world in six days, and what is contained therein, EIE, SARAYÉ, and by the power of this name PRIMEUMATON which commandeth the whole host of Heaven, curse thee, and deprive thee of thine office, joy, and place, and bind thee in the depths of the Bottomless Pit or Abyss, there to remain unto the Day of the Last Judgment. And I will bind thee in the Eternal Fire, and into the Lake of Flame and of Brimstone, unless thou comest quickly and appearest here before this Circle to do my will. Therefore, come thou! in and by the holy names ADONAI, ZABAOTH, ADONAI, AMIORAN. Come thou! for it is ADONAI who commandest thee.

IF THOU hast come thus far, and yet he appeareth not, thou mayest be sure that he is sent unto some other place by his King, and cannot come; and if it be so, invocate the King as here followeth, to send him. But if he do not come still, then thou mayest be sure that he is bound in chains in hell, and that he is not in the custody of his King. If so, and thou still hast a desire to call him even from thence, thou must rehearse the general curse which is called the Spirits' Chain.

Here followeth, therefore, the Invocation of the King:[1]

THE INVOCATION OF THE KING.

O THOU great, powerful, and mighty King AMAIMON, who bearest rule by the power of the SUPREME GOD EL over all spirits both superior and inferior of the Infernal Orders in the Dominion of the East; I do invocate and command thee by the especial and true name of GOD; and by that God that Thou Worshippest; and by the Seal of thy creation; and by the most mighty and powerful name of GOD, IEHOVAH TETRAGRAMMATON who cast thee out of heaven with all other infernal spirits; and by all the most powerful and great names of GOD who created Heaven, and Earth, and Hell, and all things in them contained; and by their power and virtue; and by the name PRIMEUMATON who commandeth the whole host of Heaven; that thou mayest cause, enforce, and compel the Spirit N. to come unto me here before this Circle in a fair and comely shape, without harm unto me or unto any other creature, to answer truly and faithfully unto all my requests; so that I may accomplish my will and desire in knowing or obtaining any matter or thing which by office thou knowest is proper for him to perform or accomplish, through the power of GOD, EL, Who created and doth dispose of all things both celestial, aërial, terrestrial, and infernal.

AFTER thou shalt have invocated the King in this manner twice or thrice over, then conjure the spirit thou wouldest call forth by the aforesaid conjurations, rehearsing them several times together, and he will come without doubt, if not at the first or second time of rehearsing. But if he do

---

[1] It will depend on the quarter to which the Spirit is attributed, which of the four chief kings is to be invoked.

not come, add the "Spirits' Chain" unto the end of the aforesaid conjurations, and he will be forced to come, even if he be bound in chains, for the chains must break off from him, and he will be at liberty:

THE GENERAL CURSE, CALLED THE SPIRITS' CHAIN, AGAINST ALL SPIRITS THAT REBEL.

O THOU wicked and disobedient spirit N., because thou hast rebelled, and hast not obeyed nor regarded my words which I have rehearsed; they being all glorious and incomprehensible names of the true GOD, the maker and creator of thee and of me, and of all the world; I DO by the power of these names the which no creature is able to resist, curse thee into the depths of the Bottomless Abyss, there to remain unto the Day of Doom in chains, and in fire and brimstone unquenchable, unless thou forthwith appear here before this Circle, in this triangle to do my will. And, therefore, come thou quickly and peaceably, in and by these names of GOD, ADONAI, ZABAOTH, ADONAI, AMIORAN; come thou! come thou! for it is the King of Kings, even ADONAI, who commandeth thee.

WHEN thou shalt have rehearsed thus far, but still he cometh not, then write thou his seal on parchment and put thou it into a strong black box;[1] with brimstone, assafœtida, and such like things that bear a stinking smell; and then bind the box up round with an iron wire, and hang it upon the point of thy sword, and hold it over the fire of charcoal; and say as followeth unto the fire first, it being placed toward that quarter whence the Spirit is to come:

THE CONJURATION OF THE FIRE.

I CONJURE thee, O fire, by him who made thee and all other creatures for good in the world, that thou torment, burn, and consume this Spirit N., for everlasting. I condemn thee, thou Spirit N., because thou art disobedient and obeyest not my commandment, nor keepest the precepts of the LORD THY GOD, neither wilt thou obey me nor mine invocations, having thereby

---

[1] This box should evidently be in metal or in something which does not take fire easily.

called thee forth, I, who am the servant of the MOST HIGH AND IMPERIAL LORD GOD OF HOSTS, IEHOVAH, I who am dignified and fortified by His celestial power and permission, and yet thou comest not to answer these my propositions here made unto thee. For the which thine averseness and contempt thou art guilty of great disobedience and rebellion, and therefore shall I excommunicate thee, and destroy thy name and seal, the which I have enclosed in this box; and shall burn thee in the immortal fire and bury thee in immortal oblivion; unless thou immediately come and appear visibly and affably, friendly and courteously here unto me before this Circle, in this triangle, in a form comely and fair, and in no wise terrible, hurtful, or frightful to me or any other creature whatsoever upon the face of earth. And thou shalt make rational answers unto my requests, and perform all my desires in all things, that I shall make unto thee.

AND if he come not even yet, thou shalt say as followeth:

THE GREATER CURSE.[1]

Now, O thou Spirit N., since thou art still pernicious and disobedient, and wilt not appear unto me to answer unto such things as I would have desired of thee, or would have been satisfied in; I do in the name, and by the power and dignity of the Omnipresent and Immortal Lord God of Hosts IEHOVAH TETRAGRAMMATON, the only creator of Heaven, and Earth, and Hell, and all that is therein, who is the marvellous Disposer of all things both visible and invisible, curse thee, and deprive thee of all thine office, joy, and place; and I do bind thee in the depths of the Bottomless Abyss there to remain until the Day of Judgment, I say into the Lake of Fire and Brimstone which is prepared for all rebellious, disobedient, obstinate, and pernicious spirits. Let all the company of Heaven curse thee! Let the sun, moon, and all the stars curse thee! Let the LIGHT and all the hosts of Heaven curse thee into the fire unquenchable, and into the torments unspeakable. And as thy name and seal contained in this box chained and bound up, shall be choked in sul-

---

[1] In some codices this is called "the Curse" only; but in one or two the "Spirits' Chain" is called "the Lesser Curse," and this the "Greater Curse."

phurous stinking substances, and burned in this material fire; so in the name IEHOVAH and by the power and dignity of these three names, TETRAGRAMMATON, ANAPHAXETON, and PRIMEUMATON, I do cast thee, O thou wicked and disobedient Spirit N., into the Lake of Fire which is prepared for the damnéd and accurséd spirits, and there to remain unto the day of doom, and never more to be remembered before the face of GOD, who shall come to judge the quick, and the dead, and the world, by fire.

THEN the exorcist must put the box into the fire, and by-and-by the Spirit will come, but as soon as he is come, quench the fire that the box is in, and make a sweet perfume, and give him welcome and a kind entertainment, showing unto him the Pentacle that is at the bottom of your vesture covered with a linen cloth, saying:

THE ADDRESS UNTO THE SPIRIT UPON HIS COMING.

BEHOLD thy confusion if thou refusest to be obedient! Behold the Pentacle of Solomon which I have brought here before thy presence! Behold the person of the exorcist in the midst of the exorcism; him who is arméd by GOD and without fear; him who potently invocateth thee and calleth thee forth unto appearance; even him, thy master, who is called OCTINOMOS. Wherefore make rational answer unto my demands, and prepare to be obedient unto thy master in the name of the Lord:

BATHAL OR VATHAT RUSHING UPON ABRAC!
ABEOR COMING UPON ABERER![1]

THEN he or they will be obedient, and bid thee ask what thou wilt, for he or they be subjected by God to fulfil our desires and commands. And when he or they shall have appeared and showed himself or themselves humble and meek, then shalt thou rehearse:

THE WELCOME UNTO THE SPIRIT.

WELCOME Spirit N., O most noble king[2] (or kings)! I say thou art welcome unto me, because I have called thee through Him who hast

[1] In the Latin, "Bathal vel Vathat super Abrac ruens! Abeor veniens super Aberer!"
[2] Or whatever his dignity may be.

created Heaven, and Earth, and Hell, and all that is in them contained, and because also thou hast obeyed. By that same power by the which I have called thee forth, I bind thee, that thou remain affably and visibly here before this Circle (or before this Circle and in this triangle) so constant and so long as I shall have occasion for thy presence; and not to depart without my licence until thou hast duly and faithfully performed my will without any falsity.

THEN standing in the midst of the Circle, thou shalt stretch forth thine hand in a gesture of command and say:

"BY THE PENTACLE OF SOLOMON HAVE I CALLED THEE! GIVE UNTO ME A TRUE ANSWER."

Then let the exorcist state his desires and requests.

And when the evocation is finished thou shalt licence the Spirit to depart thus:

THE LICENCE TO DEPART.

O THOU Spirit N., because thou hast diligently answered unto my demands, and hast been very ready and willing to come at my call, I do here licence thee to depart unto thy proper place; without causing harm or danger unto man or beast. Depart, then, I say, and be thou very ready to come at my call, being duly exorcised and conjured by the sacred rites of magic. I charge thee to withdraw peaceably and quietly, and the peace of GOD be ever continued between thee and me! AMEN!

AFTER thou hast given the Spirit licence to depart, thou art not to go out of the circle until he or they be gone, and until thou shalt have made prayers and rendered thanks unto God for the great blessings He hath bestowed upon thee in granting thy desires, and delivering thee from all the malice of the enemy the devil.

Also note! Thou mayest command these spirits into the Vessel of Brass in the same manner as thou dost into the triangle, by saying: "that thou dost forthwith appear before this Circle, in this Vessel of Brass, in a fair and comely shape," etc., as hath been shown in the foregoing conjurations.

EXPLANATION OF CERTAIN NAMES USED IN THIS BOOK LEMEGETON.[1]

Eheie. Kether.	Almighty God, whose dwelling is in the highest Heavens:
Haioth.	The great King of Heaven, and of all the powers therein:
Methratton.	And of all the holy hosts of Angels and Archangels:
Reschith.	Hear the prayers of Thy servant who putteth his trust in Thee:
Hagalgalim.	Let thy Holy Angels be commanded to assist me at this time and at all times.

Iehovah.	God Almighty, God Omnipotent, hear my prayer:
Hadonat.	Command Thy Holy Angels above the fixed stars:
Ophanim.	To be assisting and aiding Thy servant:
Iophiel.	That I may command all spirits of air, water, fire, earth, and hell:
Masloth.	So that it may tend unto Thy glory and unto the good of man.

Iehovah.	God Almighty, God Omnipotent, hear my prayer:
Elohim.	God with us, God be always present with us:
Binah.	Strengthen us and support us, both now and for ever:
Aralim.	In these our undertakings, which we perform but as instruments in Thy hands:

Zabbathi (should be Shabbathii). In the hands of Thee, the great God of Sabaoth.

Hesel (should be Chesed). Thou great God, governor and creator of the planets, and of the Host of Heaven:

Hasmalim (should be Chashmalim). Command them by Thine almighty power:

Zelez (should be Zedeq). To be now present and assisting to us Thy poor servants, both now and for ever.

[1] This explanation, or rather paraphrased prayer, only exists in one codex as far as my knowledge goes. The Qabalist will remark that the orthography of several of the Qabalistical names is incorrect. I give it, however, as it stands.—TRANS. [In any case it is worthless; the names mean nothing of the sort.—ED.]

Elohim Geber (should be Gibor). Most Almighty and eternal and ever living Lord God:

Seraphim. Command Thy seraphim:

Camael, Madim. To attend on us now at this time, to assist us, and to defend us from all perils and dangers.

Eloha. O Almighty God! be present with us both now and for ever:

Tetragrammaton. And let thine Almighty power and presence ever guard and protect us now and for ever:

Raphael. Let thy holy angel Raphael wait upon us at this present and for ever:

Schemes (or Shemesh). To assist us in these our undertakings.

Iehovah. God Almighty, God Omnipotent, hear my prayer:

Sabäoth. Thou great God of Sabäoth:

Netzah (or Netzach). All-seeing God:

Elohim. God be present with us, and let thy presence be now and alway present with us:

Haniel. Let thy holy angel Haniel come and minister unto us at this present.

Elohim. O God! be present with us, and let thy presence be now and alway present with us:

Sabäoth. O thou great God of Sabäoth, be present with us at this time and for ever:

Hodben (should be Hod simply). Let Thine Almighty power defend us and protect us, both now and for ever:

Michael. Let Michael, who is, under Thee, general of thy heavenly host:

Cochab. Come and expel all evil and danger from us both now and for ever.

Sadai. Thou great God of all wisdom and knowledge:

Jesal (should be Iesod). Instruct Thy poor and most humble servant:

Cherubim. By Thy holy cherubim:

Gabriel.   By Thy Holy Angel Gabriel, who is the Author and Messenger of good tidings:

Levanah.   Direct and support us at this present and for ever.

THE EXPLANATION OF THE TWO TRIANGLES[1] IN THE PARCHMENT.

Alpha and Omega.   Thou, O great God, Who art the beginning and the end:

Tetragrammaton.   Thou God of Almighty power, be ever present with us to guard and protect us, and let Thy Holy Spirit and presence be now and always with us:

Soluzen.   I command thee, thou Spirit, of whatsoever region thou art, to come unto this circle:

Halliza.   And appear in human shape:

Bellator (or Ballaton).   And speak unto us audibly in our mother-tongue:

Bellonoy (or Bellony).   And show, and discover unto us all treasure that thou knowest of, or that is in thy keeping, and deliver it unto us quietly:

Hallii. Hra.   And answer all such questions as we may demand without any defect now at this time.

AN EXPLANATION OF SOLOMON'S TRIANGLE.

Anephezeton.   Thou great God of all the Heavenly Host:

Primeumaton.   Thou Who art the First and Last, let all spirits be subject unto us, and let the Spirit be bound in this triangle, which disturbs[2] this place:

Michael.   By Thy Holy Angel Michael, until I shall discharge him.

(HERE ENDETH THIS FIRST BOOK OF THE LEMEGETON, WHICH IS CALLED THE GOETIA.)

---

[1] Evidently meaning both the Hexagram and the Pentagram of Solomon. (*See Figures* 155 *and* 156.)

[2] It is doubtful whether by "disturbs" is intended the Spirit or the triangle itself.

Yᵉ Conjuratiouns of ye Booke Goetia in ye Lemegeton which Solomoun ye Kynge did give unto Lemuel hys sonne, rendered into ye Magicall or Angelike Language by our Illustrious and ever-Glorious Frater, ye Wise Perdurabo, that Myghtye Chiefe of ye Rosy-Cross Fraternitye, now sepulchred in ye Vault of ye Collegium S.S. And soe may we doe alle!

ATTE YE BATHES OF ART.

Asperges me, Domine, hyssopo, et mundabor:
Lavabis me, et super nivem dealbabor.

ATTE YE INDUYNGE OF YE HOLY VESTURES.

Do-kikale vaunesa zodimezoda pire, ol aladonu na-e-el do-
In the mystery   of these   vestures of the Holy Ones, I gird up my power   in
ataraahé piamo-el od Vaoanu, do-elonusa Iaida: Ancor:
the girdles of righteousness and   truth,   in the power of the Most High :   Ancor :
Amacor: Amides: Theodonias: Anitor: Christeos micaelzodo na-e-
Amacor :   Amides :   Theodonias :   Anitor :   let be mighty   my power :
el: christeos apila: Do-elonusa Adonai, kasaremé e-karinu od
let it endure for ever :   in the power of Adonai,   to whom   the praise   and
busada tarianu lu ipamisa. AMEN.
the glory shall be; whose end cannot be.

YE FYRSTE CONJOURATIOUN.

Ol vinu od zodakame, Ilasa, Gahé N.: od elanusahé vaoresagi
I invoke and move thee, O thou, Spirit N.: and being exalted above ye

Jaida, gohusa pujo ilasa, darebesa do-o-i-apé Bera-
in the power of the Most High, I say unto thee, Obey! in the name Bera-

lanensis, Baldachiensis, Paumachia, od Apologiae Sedes: od
lanensis, Baldachiensis, Paumachia, and Apologiae Sedes: and

micaelzodo aretabasa, gahé, mire Liachidae od qouódi Salamanu
of the mighty ones who govern, spirits, Liachidae and ministers of the House

telocahé: od Cabaäme Otahila Apologiae do em Poamala, ol
of Death: and by the Chief Prince of the seat of Apologia in the Ninth Legion, I do

vinu-ta od zodaméta! Od elanusahé vaoresagi Jaida,
invoke thee and by invoking conjure thee. And being exalted above ye in the power of the Most

gohusa pujo ilasa, darebesa, do-o-i-apé totza das cameliatza od asá,
High, I say unto thee, Obey! in the name of him who spake and it was,

kasaremé tofagilo tolteregi darebesa. Pilahé Ol, das Jada oela
to whom all creatures and things obey. Moreover I, whom God made

azodiazodore Jada, das i qo-o-al marebi totza jijipahé, larinuji ilasa
in the likeness of God, who is the creator according to his living breath, stir thee up

do-o-i-apé das i salada micaelazodo Jada, El, micaelzodo od
in the name which is the voice of wonder of the mighty God, El, strong and

adapehaheta: ilasa gahé N. Od ol gohusa pujo ilasa, darebesa,
unspeakable, O thou Spirit N. And I say to thee obey,

do-o-i-apé totza das cameliatza od isa od do vomesareji do-o-i-ainu
in the name of him who spake and it was; and in every one of ye, O ye names of

Jada. Pilahé do-o-i-apé Adonai, El, Elohim, Elohi, Ehyeh Asher
God! Moreover in the names Adonai, El, Elohim, Elohi, Ehyeh Asher

Ehyeh, Zabaoth, Elion, Iah, Tetragrammaton, Shaddai, Enayo Jad
Ehyeh, Zabaoth, Elion, Iah, Tetragrammaton, Shaddai, Lord God

Iaida, ol larinuji ilasa od do-vamepelifa gohus, darebesa! ilasa
Most High, I stir thee up; and in our strength I say Obey! O

gahé N. zodameranu ca-no-quoda olé oanio; asapeta komeselahe
Spirit N. Appear unto His servants in a moment; before the circle

azodiazodore olalore od fetahé-are-zodi. Od do-o-a-ipé adapehaheta
in the likeness of a man; and visit me in peace. And in the ineffable name

Tetragrammaton Iehevohe, gohus, darebesa: soba sapahé
Tetragrammaton Iehovah, I say, Obey! whose mighty sound being

elonusahinu nazoda poilapé, zodonugonu caelazod holado, pereje
exalted in power the pillars are divided, the winds of the firmament groan aloud; the fire

je-ialaponu: caosaga zodaca do-jizodajazoda, od tofajilo Salamann
burns not; the earth moves in earthquakes; and all things of the house

pe-ripesol, od caosaji, od faorejita oresa cahisa ta jizodajazoda, od
of heaven and earth and the dwelling-place of darkness are as earthquakes, and

cahisa do-mire, od ovankaho do-koratzo. Niisa, eca, ilasa gahé N.
are in torment, and are confounded in thunder. Come forth, O Spirit N.

olé oanio: christeos faorejita afafa, imumamare laiada, od darebesa
in a moment: let thy dwelling-place be empty, apply unto us the secrets of Truth and obey

na-e-el. Niisa, fatahe-are-zodi, zodameranu pujo ooaona; zodoreje:
my power. Come forth, visit us in peace, appear unto my eyes; be friendly:

darebesa jijipahé! Lapé ol larinuji-ta do-o-i-apé Iada Uaoanu das
Obey the living breath! For I stir thee up in the name of the God of Truth who

apila, Helioren. Darebesa jijipahe, eca, do-miame pujo valasa,
liveth for ever, Helioren. Obey the living breath, therefore continually unto the end

ta anugelareda: zodameranu ooaona: zodoreje: gohola laiada
as my thoughts appear to my eyes: therefore be friendly: speaking the secrets

do-bianu od do-omepe!
of Truth in voice and in understanding.

YE SECOUNDE CONJOURATIOUN

Ol vinu ilesa, od zodakame ilasa, od larinuji ilasa, ilasa gahé N:
I invoke thee, and move thee, and stir thee up O Spirit N

zodameranu pujo-ooaona asapeta komeselahe azodiazodore olalore;
appear unto my eyes before the circle in the likeness of a man

dooaipé od quo-o-a-ipé Iah od Vau, das Adam cameliatza: od
in the names and by the name   Iah and Vau,   which Adam   spake   and

do-o-a-ipé Iada, Agla, das Lot cameliatza: od asa ta obelisonugi
in the name of God,   Agla, which Lot   spake: and it was as pleasant deliverers

pujo-totza od totza salamanu: od do-o-a-ipé Ioth das Iakob
unto him   and his   house   and in the name Ioth which Iacob

cameliatza, do-bianu Piré das adarepanu totza, od asata
spake   in the voice of the Holy ones who cast him down, and it was also

obelisonuji do vanupehe Esau totza e-si-asacahé: od do-o-a-ipé
as pleasant deliverers in the anger of his brother   and in the name

Anaphareton das Aaron cameliatza od asa ta ananael: od do-o-a-ipé
Anaphaxeton, which Aaron   spake   and it was as the Secret Wisdom and in the name

Zabaoth das Mosheh cameliatza, od tofajilo zodinu asa ta kanila: od
Zabaoth which Mosheh   spake,   and all things of water were as blood; and

do-o-a-ipé Asher Ehyeh Oriston, das Mosheh cameliatza od tofajilo
in the name Asher Ehyeh Oriston, which Mosheh   spake,   and all

zodinu asa polaki hami das vaugeji das goholore pujo salamanu, das
waters were bringing forth creatures who wax strong, which lifted up unto the houses, which

quasabé tofajilo: od do-o-a-ipé Elion, das Mosheh cameliatza, od asa
destroy all things and in the name of Elion which Mosheh   spake,   and it was as

oreri caelazod coresa ta asage do homila Ipame caosago od
stones from the firmament of wrath, such as was not in the ages of Time the beginning of the Earth

do-o-a-ipé Adni, das Mosheh cameliatza od zodameranu hami caosago,
and in the name of Adni, which Mosheh spake and there appeared creatures of earth

das quasabé das oreri ge-poilape: od do-o-a-ipé Schema Amathia, das
who destroyed what the big stones did not: and in the name Schema Amathia, which

Ioshua vinu od rore pa-aotza vaoresaji ili-i tahila Gibeon od
Ioshua invoked, and the Sun remained over ye, O ye hills the seats of Gibeon, and

do-o-a-ipé Alpha od Omega, das Daniel cameliatza, od quasabe Bel
in the names Alpha and Omega which Daniel   spake,   and destroyed Bel

od Uovina: od do-o-a-ipé Emmanuel das Nore Iada oekarimi
and the Dragon: and in the name Emmanuel which the sons of God sang praises

notahoa Ialapereji, od ca-ca-come do-zodilodarepe: od do-o-a-ipé
in the midst of the burning plain, and flourished in conquest: and in the name

Hagios: od do-tahila Adni: od do Ischyros, Athanatos, Paracletos:
Hagios, and by the Throne of Adni, and in Ischyros, Athanatos, Paracletos:

od do O Theos, Ictros, Athanatos. Od do vaunesa omaoasa laiada
and in O Theos, Ictros, Athanatos. And in these names of secret truth,
Agla, On, Tetragrammaton, vinu ol od zodame ilasa. Od do
Agla, On, Tetragrammaton, do I invoke and move thee. And in
vaunesa omaoasa, od tofajilo das cahisa do-o-a-inu Jada laiada
these names, and all things that are the names of the God of Secret Truth
das apila, Ja-i-don. Ol vinu od larinuji ilasa, Ilasa gahé N.
who liveth for ever, the All-Powerful. I invoke and stir thee up, O spirit N.
nomiji do totza das goho od asa, casareme tofajilo tol-
Even by him who spake and it was, to whom all creatures
toregi darebesa: od do balatune od vaunupehe Jada: od do
are obedient and in the Extreme Justice and Anger of God; and by the
zodimibe das i asapeta basada Jada, micaelzodo; od ji: do toltoreji
veil (?) that is before the glory of God, mighty; and by the creatures
jijipahe asapata otahila soba ooaona cahisa ra-as od bolanu: do
of living breath before the Throne whose eyes are east and west; by
perejé do iala-pire-gahé otahila: do pire peripesol: od do ananael
the fire in the fire of just Glory of the Throne; by the Holy ones of Heaven; and by the secret
Jada: Elonusahé larinuji ilasa ol: zodameranu asapeta vaunesa
wisdom of God, I, exalted in power, stir thee up. Appear before this
komeselahe; darebesa do tofajilo das gohus: do emetajisa Basdathea
circle; obey in all things that I say; in the seal Basdathea
Baldachia: od do vaunesa do-o-a-inu Primeumaton, das Mosheh
Baldachia; and in this Name Primeumaton, which Mosheh
cameliatza, od caosaji poilape, od Korah, Dathan, od Abiram Ionukaho
spake, and the earth was divided, and Korah, Dathan, and Abiram fell
pi-adapehé. Eca darebesa do-tofajilo ilasa gahé N. darebesa go-a-
in the depth. Therefore obey in all things, O spirit N., obey thy crea-
anu. Niisa, ilasa; zodameranu pujo-ooaona felathe-are-zodi;
tion. Come thou forth: appear unto my eyes; visit us in peace,
zodoreje: niisa ole oanio: darebesa na-e-el, gohola laiada
be friendly; come forth in the 24th of a moment; obey my power, speaking the secrets of
Do-bianu od do-omepe.
Truth in voice and in understanding!

YE CONSTRAYNTE.

Ol larinuji-ilasa ilasa gahé N. do tofjila das kahisa do-o-a-inu busada
I stir thee up, O spirit N. in all things that are the names of glory

od mikaelzodo. Jada Darisapa das i darilapi omepe, Adni Ihvh
and power of God the Great One who is greater than understanding, Adni Ihvh

Tzabaoth: niisa ole oanio: christeos faorejita afafa; imimuamare
Tzabaoth, come forth in the 24th of a moment; let Thy dwelling-place be empty; apply thyself unto

laiada od dorebesa na-e-el: zodamerann pujo-ooaona fetahe-are-
the secret truth and obey my power: appear unto my eyes, visit us in peace,

zodi, gohola laiada do-bianu od do-omepe. Ol larinuji-ilasa od
speaking the secrets of truth in voice and understanding. I stir thee up and

zodakame ilasa gahé N. do tofjila do-o-a-inu ds goho i eli: od ol
move thee, O spirit N., in all the names that I have said, and I

vamuela vaunesa ela od norezoda do-o-a-inu quiinu Solomon, enayo
add these one and six names wherein Solomon, the lord

ananael, aala amiranu gahé vimé, do-podizodopé Adni
of the secret wisdom, placed yourselves, spirits of wrath, in a vessel, Adonai,

Preyai Tetragrammaton, Anaphareton Inessenfatoal Pathtomon od
Preyai Tetragrammaton, Anaphaxeton Inessenfatoal, Pathtomon and

Itemon: zodameranu as apeta vaunesa comerelahe: darebesa do
Itemon: appear before this circle; obey in

tofjila na-e-el. Od ta ilasa iehe totza das je-dare-pasa od je-niisa,
all things my power. And as thou art he that obeys not and comes not

ol tarianu, do-na-e-el O Jada Jaida das apila, soba i go-o-al tofjilo
I shall be in thy power, O God Most High that liveth for ever, who is the creator of all things

do-norezoda basajime, Eie, Saraye, od do-na-e-el do-o-i-apé
in six days Eie, Saraye, and in my power in the name

Primeumaton das bojira voresa proamal peripesol, Amema ilasa, od
Primeumaton that ruleth over the palaces of heaven, Curse Thee, and

quasahé otahila, mozod, od elonusa, od ol commemahé ilasa pi-
destroy thy seat, joy, and power; and I bind thee in

adapehe Abaddon, pa-aolza kakareji besajinu zodizodarasa soba lu
the depth of Abaddon, to remain until the day of judgment whose end

ipamisa. *Od commemahé do pereje salabarotza kynutzire faboanu,*
cannot be. And I bind thee in the fire of sulphur mingled with poison
od zodumebi pereii od salabarotza: niisa, eca, dorebesa na-e-el od
and the seas of fire and sulphur: come forth, therefore, obey my power and
zodameranu asapeta vaunesa komesalohé. Eca, niisa, do-o-i-apé
appear before this circle. Therefore come forth in the name
pire Adni, Zabaoth, Adonai, Amioran. Niisa! lapé zodiredo Adni
of the Holy Ones Zabaoth, Adonai, Amioran. Come! for I am Adonai
das larinuji elasa.
who stir thee up.

YE POTENT INVOCATIOUN OF HYS KYNGE.

Ilasa darisapa, micaelzodo, tabaame, Amaimon,[1] das bojira alonusahi
O thou great powerful governor Amaimon,[1] who reigneth exalted in the
Jaida El voresa tofijilo gahé do elonu-dohe Ra-As,
power of the only El above all spirits in the kingdoms of the East,
(Babaje, Bobanu, Lucala,) ol vinu od zodakame ilasa do-o-a-ipé
(South, West, North), I invoke and move thee in the name of
vaoanu Mada, od do Mada soba ilasa iehe boaluahe: od do
the true God, and in God whom thou worshippest: and in
Emetâjisa qoaänu: od do-o-a-ipe micaelzodo Mada, Iehevohe
the seal of thy creation: and in the mighty names of God, Iehevohe
Tetragrammaton das adarepanu ilasa peripesol, ilasa od gahé
Tetragrammaton, who cast thee down from Heaven, thou and the spirits of
oresa: od do-o-a-ipe tofijilo micaelzodo Mada das i quo-á-al peripesol,
darkness, and in all the names of the mighty God who is the creator of Heaven
od caosagi, od faorejita oresa, od tofijilo; od do uo elonusa od
and earth, and the dwelling of darkness, and all things and in their power and
lukiftias; od do-o-a-ipe Primeumaton das bojua voresa pooumala
brightness; and in the name Primeumaton who reigns over the palaces
peripesol: Polakame, gohus, gahé N., Polakame totza ole oanio:
of Heaven. Bring forth, I say, the spirit N.; bring him forth in the 24th of a moment

---
[1] Or Gaap, Paimon, Zodimay, as the case may be.

christeos totza faorejita afafa; kakareji fetabe-are-zodi gobola
let his dwelling be empty until he visit us in peace, speaking the

laiada: kakareji dorebasa na-e-el od totza quaa, elonusahi Mada, El,
secrets of truth; until he obey my power and his creation in the power of God, El,

das i quo-o-al sa das larasada tofijilo; peripesol, caelazod, caosago,
who is the Creator and doth dispose of all things, heaven, firmament, earth,

od faorejita oresa.
and the dwelling of darkness.

YE GENERALL CURSE.

Yclept ye Spirits' Chayne, agaynste all Spirits yᵀ rebelle.

Ilasa babalonu gahe N. das ge-dorebesa, bajilenu oborela, od vinu
O thou wicked spirit N. that obeyeth not, because I made a law and invoked

omaosa busada od adapehaheta Mada Cooanu go-a-al tofijilo, od ilas
the names of the glorious and ineffable God of Truth, the creator of all, and thou

ge-dorebesa sapahe das gohas: eca ol amema ilasa pi-adapahe
obeyest not the mighty sounds that I make: therefore I curse thee in the depth

Abaddon pa-aotza kakoreji besajinu zodizodarasa do-mire, do-pereji
of Abaddon to remain until the day of judgment in torment in fire

od do salaberotza ds lu ipamisa, kakareji ilas zodameranu asapeta
and in sulphur without end, until thou appear before

kromeselahe od dorebesa na-e-el. Miisa, eca, ole oanio, asapeta
our will and obey my power. Come, therefore, in the 24th of a moment, before

komesalahe do i-be-da, do-o-o-ape vaunesa, od quo-o-i-ape Mada
the circle in the triangle in this name and by this name of God,

Adni, Tzabaoth, Adonai, Amioran. Miisa! Miisa! lape Enayo
Adni, Tzabaoth, Adonai, Amioran. Come! Come! for it is the Lord

Enayo, Adonai, das larinuji-ilasa.
of Lords Adni, that stirreth thee up.

YE CONJOURATIOUN OF YE FYRE.

Ol larinuji, ilasa pereje, do totza das i qo-o-ala-ilasa od tofijila
I stir thee up, O thou fire, in him who is thy Creator and of all
tol-toreji: mire, ialaponu, quasabe gabe N. paida soba lu ipamis: ol
creatures. Torment, burn, destroy the spirit N. always whose end cannot be,
ad peranuta ilasa do zodizodarasa s do balatime, ilasa gabe N.,
I judge thee in judgment and in extreme justice, O spirit N.,
bajilenu iehe totza ds ge-darebesa na-e-el, od ge-darebesa das oborela
because thou art he that obeyeth not my power and obeyeth not that law which
amayo Mada, od ge-llarebesa sapabe od jijipabe, das ol vinu,
the Lord God made, and obeyeth not the Mighty Sounds and the Living Breath which I invoke,
das gobus: Niisa, ol, das zodiredo Moco Jaida Cabaame Enayo
which I send: Come forth, I, who am the Servant of the Same Most High governor Lord
Jad micaelzodo, Jehovohe, ol das zodiredo elonusabe, das zodivedo
God powerful, Iehovohe, I who am exalted in power and am
micaelzodi do totza elonusa vaoresagi, ilasa das ge-niisabe daluga
mighty in his power above ye, O thou who comest not giving
adana gono iadapiel das hometobe. Eca gobus zodizodearasa: ol
obedience and faith to him that liveth and triumpheth. Therefore I say the judgment: I
amema-ta, od quasaba dooain N od ametajisa N. das oali do vaunesa
curse thee and destroy the name N. and the seal N., which I have placed in this
faorejita faboanu od ol ialaponu ilasa do pereje soba lu ipamis od
dwelling of poison, and I burn thee in fire whose end cannot be; and
adarepanu ilasa pi-adapebe mire, sobame voresa ilasa ge-torezodul:
I cast thee down unto the seas of torment, out of which thou shalt not rise
kakareji niisa pajo-ooaoanu: fetabe are-zodi: zodoreje ca-ol asapeta
until thou come to my eyes: visit me in peace: be friendly before
komeselabe, do i-be-da, ole, oanio azodiazodore olalore, ge-kiaisi
the circle in the Δ in the 24th of a moment in the likeness of a man not unto the
nore-mo-lape, tol-toregi, q-tofajilo voresa adoianu caosago. Dorebesa
terror of the sons of men the creatures or all things on the face of the earth. Obey
na-e-el, marebe koredazodizoda, dorebesa jijipabe, oborela das gobus.
my power like reasoning creatures; obey the living breath, the law which I speak.

YE GRETER CURSE.

Sola-bi-enu, Madariitza! Ilasa gahé N. basilenu iehe totza das
Hearken to me, O ye Heavens! O thou Spirit N. because thou art the disobedient

ge-dorebesa das i babalonu, od ge-zodameranu gohola liaida marebe
one who is wicked and appearest not, speaking the secrets of truth according to

isipahé: Ol, elonusahe Diada, Ia-i-don Elazodape komesalahe,
the living breath: I, exalted in the power of God, the All-powerful, the centre of the circle,

micaelazodo Mada das apila lu ipamis, Iehevohe Tetragrammaton,
powerful God who liveth, whose end cannot be, Iehevohe Tetragrammaton,

ela go-a-al pe-ripesol, caosago, od faoresita oresa, od tofajilo das
the only creator of heaven, earth, and dwelling of darkness and all that is in

cahisa do-no poamala, das larasada do-ananael tofajilo do-oresa
their palaces; who disposeth in secret wisdom of all things in darkness

sa-do-lukiftiasa: Amema ilasa od adarepanu-ilasa, od quasabé
and in light: Curse thee and cast thee down and destroy

otahila, mozod, od elonusa, od ol commemahe pi-adapahé Abaddon,
thy seat, joy and power, and I bind thee in the depths of Abaddon,

pa-aotza kakaresi basajinu zodi-zodarasa soba lu ipamisa, gohus,
to remain until the day of judgment whose end cannot be, I say,

pujo-zodumebi peresi od salaberotza, das aberamisi pujo-babalonu
unto the seas of fire and sulphur which I have prepared for the wicked

gahé, das ge-dorebesa, nore madarida.
spirits that obey not; the sons of iniquity.

> **Christeos coremefa peripesol amema ilasa!**
> Let the company of heaven curse thee!
>
> **Christeos roray, geraa, tofajilo aoiveae amema ilasa!**
> Let the sun, moon, all the stars curse thee!
>
> **Christeos lukiftias od tofajilo pire peripesol amema ilasa, pujo**
> Let the light and all the Holy Ones of Heaven curse thee unto

iala-peresi das apila, od pujo mire adâpehabeta!
the burning flame that liveth for ever, and unto the torment unspeakable!

Od nomiji dooain od ametajisa, das oali do-vaunesa faorejita
And even as thy name and seal, which I have put in this dwelling of

faboanu, larianu do-mire nofahon toltoregi salaberotza od jirosabe,
poison, shall be in torment among creatures of sulphur and bitter sting,

olapireta do-pereji caosago: do-o-a-ipe Jehevohe od elonusahe do-
burning in fire of earth, in them Iehevohe and exalted in power in

vaunesa dooainu dau, Tetragrammaton, Anaphareton, od
these three names, Tetragrammaton Anaphaxeton,

Primeumaton, Ol adarepanu ilasa gahe babalonu N. pujo-zodumebi
Primeumaton, I cast thee down, O wicked spirit N. unto the seas

perejela od salabaiotza, das abaramiji pujo-babalonu gahe das ge-
of fire and sulphur which are prepared for the wicked spirits that

dorebesa, nore-madarida, pa-iotza kakareji basajinu zodizodarasa;
obey not, the sons of iniquity, to remain until the day of judgment;

bamesa-ilasa Okada jehusozoda; adoianu Diada bamesa adoianu N.
let the Mercies of God forget thee; let the face of God forget the face of N.

das iparanu lukiftias, Jada bamesa, gohus, das tarianu piape balata
who will not see light: let God forget, I say that shall be the balance of justice

voresa nore jijipahe od telokake od caosagi, do-pereji.
over the sons of living breath and death and the world, by fire.

YE ADDRESSE UNTO YE SPIRIT ON HYS COMING.

Micama! Ol O vaukaho ilasa ta iehe totza das ge-darebesa!
Behold! I confound thee as thou art he that obeys not!

Micama kikale emetajisa Solomon das ol polakame pujo ji-mi-
Behold the mysteries of the seal of Solomon which I bring forth unto thy power and

caelazod! Micama go-a-al, elzodape komeselake jijipahe; totza das
presence! Behold the creator, the centre of the circle of the living breath; he that

i elanusahe Mada od iparanu kiaisi: totza das micaelzodo vinu
is exalted in the power of God and shall not see unto the terror: he that powerfully invoketh

od larinuji-ilasa pujo ooaona: totza, enayo de genetaahe, soba
and stirreth thee up unto visible appearance: he, the lord of thy governments whose

Dooain Ivaumeda Octinomos.
Name is called Octinomos.

Dorebesa, eca, na-e-el, ta koredazodizod, do-o-a-ipe enayo:
Obey, therefore, my power as a reasoning creature in the name of the Lord.

Bathat vel Uathat super Abrac Ruens!
Abeor veniens super Aberer!

YE WELLCOME UNTO Y^E SPIRIT DYGNYTIE.

Ol zodiredo totza das i dorepehala pujo ilasa, ilasa gahe ... N. turebesa
I am he that is looking with gladness upon thee, O thou spirit ... N.[1] beautiful

od akarinu! dorepehela, gohus, bajileim iehe ivaumed do totza
and praiseworthy! with gladness I say, because thou art called in him

das i qo-o-al peripesol, od caosago, od faorejita oresa, od tofajilo
who is creator of Heaven and earth and the dwelling of darkness, and all things

das cahisa do-no poamala, od bajilenu iehe noco adana.
that are in their palaces, and because thou art the servant of obedience.

Do vaunesa elonusa kasaremeji dorebesa jijipahé, ol commennahe
In these the power by which thou art obedient to the living breath, I bind

ilasa, pa-iotz a puje-ooaona gi-mi-caelaz ta noco gono asapeta
thee to remain visible to our eyes in power and presence as the servant of fealty before the

komesalehé kakareji gohus "Uaunilaji pujo-faorejita" kakareji
circle until I say "Descend unto thy dwelling" until the

jijipahé bianu enayo i mariehé oholera das tarianu ivalugame
living breath of the voice of the Lord is according to the law which shall be given

pujo-ilasa.
unto thee.

Do-emetajisa ananael Solomonis iehe ivaunieda!
By the seal of the secret wisdom of Solomon thou art called!

---

[1] Knights—pu-imé. Prelates—tabaame. Earls—nazodapesad. Kings—roré. Dukes—oheloka. Presidents—balazodareji. Marquises—geraa.

Dorebesa sapahé! dorebesa jijipahé bianu Enayo!
Obey the mighty sounds! obey the living breath of the voice of the Lord!

Follows ye charge.

YE LICENCE TO YE SPIRIT Y^r HE MAYE DEPART.

Ilasa gahé N. bajilenu iehe noco gono adana od bajilenu iehe
O thou Spirit N.   because   thou art the servant of fealty and obedience, and because
totza das dorebesa na-e-el od qua-a-on; eca gohusa: Caunilagi
thou art he that obeyeth my power and thy creation; therefore I say   Descend unto
pujo-faoregita dorepesa oborela das e-ola, ge-kiaisi nore-mo-lapi,
  thy dwelling,   obey   the law which I have made, without terror to the sons of men,
tol-toregi, tofajilo voresa adoranu caosago.
  creatures, all things upon the surface of the earth.

    Caunilagi, eca, gohus, od bolape ta balozodareji kokasa: niisa
  Descend therefore   I say,   and be thou   as stewards   of Time; come forth
paida ole oanio, nonuji quonu das toatare bianu Enayo; ole
  in a moment,   even   as servants that hearken to the voice of the Lord; in the
oanio kasaremeji ol vinu ilasa od larinuji ilasa od zodakame ilas
moment   in which   I invoke thee   and   stir thee up   and   move thee
do-kikakle ananael Mo-a-al!
in the mysteries of the secret wisdom of the Creator!

    Caunilagi pujo-faorijita do-quasahi: christeos Iehusozod Diada
  Descend unto thy dwelling place in pleasure: let there be   the mercies   of God
voresa ilasa: zodoreje do-miamé solamianu tarianu beliora pujo-
  upon thee: be friendly in continuing; whose long continuance shall be comforters
tolahamé. Amen.
unto all creatures. Amen.